Planting Seeds

A Collection Of Sermon Starter Sketches

Jill Lamkin

CSS Publishing Company, Inc., Lima, Ohio

PLANTING SEEDS

The original purchaser may photocopy material in this publication for use as it was intended (worship material for worship use; educational material for classroom use; dramatic material for staging or production). No additional permission is required from the publisher for such copying by the original purchaser only. Inquiries should be addressed to: Permissions, CSS Publishing Company, Inc., P.O. Box 4503, Lima, Ohio 45802-4503.

Scripture quotations are from the New American Standard Bible, © 1960, 1962, 1963, 1968, 1971, 1972, 1973, 1975, 1977 by The Lockman Foundation. Used by permission.

For more information about CSS Publishing Company resources, visit our website at www.csspub.com or email us at custserv@csspub.com or call (800) 241-4056.

Cover design by Jenna Brannon/Barbara Spencer
ISBN 0-7880-2375-6
PRINTED IN U.S.A.

*To Judi Daniels, my friend and my inspiration,
and to the drama teams
at Warehouse Christian Ministries, Roseville
and Harvest Valley Christian Church, Pleasanton*

Table Of Contents

Preface

One Easter morning, I stood in a choir looking out over the congregation. God whispered to me, "Look at their faces." Some were joyfully worshiping. Some were broken and weeping. Some looked bored. Others stood, arms crossed; the resentment at being dragged to church for Easter etched on their faces. God whispered again, "They've come for so many different reasons, but they've all come. Tell them that I love them," and my passion and calling to tell his story, through drama, began.

My hope and my continual prayer is that God will use these dramas to connect with the disconnected, to reach into guarded hearts to plant seeds of truth, and to create receptivity for the sermon that follows. As you perform these dramas, I pray God will open hearts in your congregation so that you will have the opportunity to tell them how much he loves them.

A Gift From My Father

Each believer is given gifts from our Heavenly Father. These gifts enable us to bring the living water of Christ to those thirsty ones around us. In "A Gift From My Father," a woman discovers her gift from her Father is exactly what is needed to bring the water of life to a thirsty traveler.

Cast

Thirsty One — is thirsty from his travels (may also be played by a woman)

Woman — wants to help the traveler, but until she realizes what she holds in her hand, she sees no way to do it

Setting And Costumes

The drama takes place beside a well that has a rope, but no bucket.

Both characters are dressed in hiking clothes. The clothes are light-colored so that attention is focused on the darker colored jar.

Props

A well with a rope attached, but no bucket at the rope's end

A dark-colored clay jar or jug with a handle that can be tied to a rope

---

(Woman stands beside a well. She holds a clay jug or jar. She holds it close to her body with both hands. Thirsty One enters. He has walked far and is thirsty.)

Thirsty One: Is this the well?

Woman: Yes.

Thirsty One: Is it deep?

9

Woman: It's deep and cold and crystal clear.

Thirsty One: *(looks longingly into the well, reaches down into it with his hands, but comes up without water; sighs, then notices the jar Woman holds)* What do you have in your hands?

(Woman holds the jar out in her hands to show him.)

Thirsty One: What is it?

Woman: I'm not sure. I've always had it, and I carry it with me because I know it has a use.

Thirsty One: *(growing weak from thirst, steadies himself against the well)* Where did you get it?

Woman: It was a gift from my Father. *(notices his weakness)* Are you all right?

Thirsty One: I'm so thirsty. *(sinks down to the ground and leans against well)*

Woman: When did you have water last?

Thirsty One: It was ... I can't remember. I found a small pool of water a few days ago, but it was stagnant. The water was polluted. *(looks again at the jar Woman holds)* Your gift from your Father, it looks like it was handmade. Is it his work?

Woman: Yes, my Father made it for me. It was his gift to me the day I was born.

Thirsty One: *(very weak)* What do you do with it?

Woman: Mostly I decorate with it. I set it on my shelf when I'm at home. When I go out, I carry it around to try to figure out its purpose.

(Thirsty One slumps over)

Woman: *(bends down over him)* Are you okay? I'm going to find some help. I'll try to find a way to bring you water.

(Woman looks frantically around her and then looks down at the jar she holds. The look on her face changes to a look of revelation and discovery. She quickly takes the jar to the well, ties it to the rope, lowers it down, and pulls it back up. She carries it as though it is heavy with water. She lifts the Thirsty One's head and helps him to drink. He revives enough to hold the jar on his own and drink deeply of the water.)

How's Your Vision?

When our spiritual vision needs adjustment, we can't see past the end of our noses, and often we don't want to. God wants to expand our vision, but sometimes we resist and want to keep wearing our old pair of glasses.

Cast
Salesperson — may be played by a man or a woman — is helpful and increasingly concerned for his/her customer
Mr. Gray — can't and doesn't want to see past the end of his nose

Setting And Costumes
The lens and frames shop at an ophthalmologist's office
Salesperson wears a lab coat

Props
Pairs of glasses displayed on a stand as in an optometry office
Two additional pairs of glasses
Table
Eye chart
Large makeup mirror to stand on the table
Papers to serve as medical records
Two sets of keys

———————

(Salesperson enters and begins arranging the pairs of eyeglasses on the table. An eye chart is behind the table. Mr. Gray enters wearing a pair of glasses and walks up to the table.)

Salesperson: Oh, hello, Mr. Gray. I have your new glasses right here. If you want to have a seat, we can see if they need any adjustments.

Mr. Gray: Thank you. *(sits down)*

Salesperson: *(puts the glasses in front of him)* Here they are.

(Mr. Gray feels around on the table as if he can't see the glasses.)

Salesperson: *(puts the glasses in his hand and looks puzzled)* Right here, Sir.

Mr. Gray: Oh, thank you. *(takes off his old glasses)*

(As Mr. Gray is getting ready to put on the new glasses, Salesperson puts a mirror in front of him.)

Mr. Gray: *(puts on the glasses, sees the mirror, and gives a startled jump at his reflection)* Who is that?

Salesperson: Well, that's you, Sir. It's your reflection in the mirror.

Mr. Gray: *(takes off new glasses and puts on the old ones then moves the mirror toward him until it is touching his nose)* You're right. This is me. *(continues to stare at himself in the mirror, forgetting anyone else is there, until Salesperson speaks again)*

Salesperson: Mr. Gray, why don't you try your new glasses again?

Mr. Gray: Oh, okay. *(puts on new glasses, looks around hesitantly, then takes them off and puts on the old glasses)* I'm sorry. I just don't think these will work.

Salesperson: If the frames are uncomfortable, I can adjust them for you.

Mr. Gray: No ... no, the frames are fine. I don't like the strength of the lenses.

Salesperson: Sir, these glasses were made from the prescription your ophthalmologist wrote.

Mr. Gray: I think I'll keep using my old glasses. I'm used to them.

Salesperson: You're used to them? Mr. Gray, with these new glasses on you will have 20/20 vision. *(picks up a paper)* Your ophthalmologist's report says with your old glasses you can see clearly ... *(reading from the paper)* to the end of your nose. Sir, I'm confident these new glasses will give you a whole new life.

Mr. Gray: That's just it. I don't want a whole new life. I really like my old life.

Salesperson: *(not scolding, but very curious)* You're telling me you like not being able to see past the end of your nose?

Mr. Gray: I don't know if I like it. But ... it's comfortable.

Salesperson: Comfortable?

Mr. Gray: When I get home, I can't see my lawn. I don't know if it needs mowing. So I don't mow it. I can't see if my neighbor's car is broken down on the side of the road ... so I don't need to help him. I can't see myself in the mirror ... except for my nose, so I don't need to worry about exercising.

Salesperson: Sir, you know there are people whose eyesight is not correctable who live very full lives. Your vision, on the other hand, is very correctable, but you choose to wear your old glasses. I don't understand.

Mr. Gray: *(shrugs)* These old glasses are comfortable. *(stands to go and pulls car keys from pocket)*

Salesperson: *(alarmed)* You didn't drive here ... those aren't your car keys are they?

Mr. Gray: *(holds the keys very close to his eyes to see them and finally shakes his head)* No, these are my wife's keys. I hide them from her. Her eyes aren't so good anymore. I don't think she should be driving. *(reaches into pocket and pulls out another set of keys)* *These* are my car keys. *(exits after bumping into a few things)*

Salesperson: *(stands there not believing what he/she is seeing, finally exits after him calling)* Mr. Gray!

Lights out

Monologue For A Traveler

This old traveler of life's path tells of the day he discovered that those footsteps behind him weren't to be feared. In fact, they were the footsteps of Goodness and Mercy sent by the Lord himself to follow him on his journey. The traveler carries an invitation. He is going to the house of the Lord where he has been invited to live forever. "Monologue For A Traveler" is based on God's promises to us in Psalm 23. It can be used with messages on fear, anxiety about the future, and the promises of God's care for us.

Cast

A seventyish-year-old man or woman who conveys a deep trust in God and never tires of telling about the invitation to live with him forever. *(Can be played by a person of any age if makeup is used to make the person appear seventy years old.)*

Setting And Costumes

A backdrop showing a path through a forest gives the feeling of journeying with the traveler, however, the monologue can be performed on an empty stage.

The man or woman is dressed in khaki or brownish colored walking clothes and wears hiking boots. Makeup may be needed to make the actor appear older.

Props

Walking stick
Piece of paper

(The traveler enters carrying a walking stick, and addresses the audience.)

I've been on this journey for seventy years, and I have to tell you, I used to wake up every morning scared to death. You see, I never knew what was ahead. Still don't know. How could I? Every day I'm going somewhere I've never been before. *(quiet for a moment and then pulls something from a pocket)* Did I tell you where I'm headed? I have an invitation. *(opens it and reads aloud)* To live in the house of the Lord forever. *(closes the invitation)* Forever! Can you believe that? This path ends right at the door of his house. *(puts the invitation away)* I never get tired of reading that invitation. *(quiet again)*

Oh, but like I was saying, this path used to scare me to death. One day ... it was a really dark day, almost nighttime ... I was zigzagging across the trail from tree to tree, hiding behind each one before dashing to the next, *(acts this out while describing it)* when I heard footsteps ... behind me ... following me. I'd heard them before on dark nights. I took a few steps *(takes a few steps)* and the feet took a few steps. I stopped *(stops)* and they stopped. Finally, I stopped completely and flattened myself against a tree hoping to lose them, *(acts this out)* and you'll never believe what happened. Two strangers appeared and introduced themselves. Called themselves Goodness and Mercy. Said they'd been following me since I began the journey. Sent by the Lord himself to escort me to his house.

I asked why I'd never seen them before ... *(amazed)* and they said I had seen them before, many times, but each time they looked different. Goodness said he was the one who took me in and fed me the night I wandered off the path. Mercy said she was the one who pardoned me when I couldn't pay a debt. *(laughs)* I had been running scared from the footsteps of Goodness and Mercy. There was not a moment they hadn't been with me, not a day in the future they wouldn't be following me.

Now each new day is not so frightening. In fact, I wake up in the morning looking forward to the journey *(smiles)* and looking forward to my destination. *(pulls out the invitation)* Did I tell you I have an invitation — *(exits while looking at invitation, then pauses and reads invitation again with awe)* to live in the house of the Lord ... forever.

Look At That!

"Look At That!" is a look at coveting. Discontentment and pettiness arise in these neighbors' hearts as they assess and grow jealous of each other based on appearance and possessions.

Cast

Woman — wife who thinks her own life isn't good enough — wants more and blames her husband for the lack

Man — husband who also wants what he doesn't have

Daughter — teenage daughter of the couple — a little immature and whiny

Neighbor Woman — new neighbor moving in next door

Neighbor Man — new neighbor moving in next door

Setting And Costumes

Woman and Man stand facing audience and with one finger pretend to bend one of the slats of a mini-blind down to peek out at the new neighbors. Three chairs or a small couch are on stage.

Everyone is dressed casually. It's a Saturday, and no one has anything to do but move furniture or spy on the neighbors.

Props

Three chairs or small couch

A plate of cookies

———————

(Woman peeks through her window so as not to be seen by the new neighbors.)

Woman: Look at that furniture.

Man: *(entering the room)* Where?

Woman: Right there. *(points out the window)* They just took it out of the moving truck. *(they watch out the window)* Do you recognize it?

Man: No.

Woman: *(a little irritated)* It's the same set I want from Spensers. Remember? You said we couldn't afford it.

Man: I said we could get the set just like it at Furniture World: the one that's $1,500 cheaper.

Woman: *(shakes her head and rolls her eyes in disgust)* I want that set. *(pointing out the window)*

Man: *(shrugs and keeps looking out the window)* How much do you think they paid for that house?

Woman: *(looking around her own house)* More than we paid for this one. Did you see how that guy was dressed last week when he met the realtor over there? Really expensive suit. *He* must be making money. *(glances sideways at Man)*

Man: *(clenches his jaw)* I heard they bought it as a fixer-upper. Probably got a good deal.

Woman: *(sarcastically)* Must be tough. A five-bedroom, three-car garage fixer-upper with a gourmet kitchen, a pool ... *(angry look at Man)* and a spa ... and a Jacuzzi in the master-*suite*. *(looks around her own house again)* Must be tough.

Man: Just give me some time. We only moved in last month. How do you know what that house is like inside anyway?

Woman: I read the flyer on the realtor's sign. Wanted to know what we were up against.

Man: So what was the price?

Woman: It didn't say. Just gave the number to call for more information. That means it's expensive.

Man: Wow, look at that weight machine. That's the one I want. Remember the infomercial? *(starts to pump weights and flex his muscles in imitation)* Oh. *(drooling — not really — just sounds like he might start)* There's the squat rack. He even has the Olympic barbell set. *(whining)* And look at those free weights. Look at th... Look at his wife! She's carrying that fifty-pound stack of weights. Maybe she's the one who works out. Look at her. She's in great shape. *(His wife glares at him, but he misses it. His back is to her.)* Maybe she'd let you work out with her. *(Another angry glare at his back. The wife has moved back from the window. She looks down at herself, sucks in her stomach and compares herself to the neighbor. She sits down in a chair.)*

Daughter: *(enters the room)* What are you looking at?

Woman: New neighbors.

Daughter: They have any kids? Like an eighteen-year-old son with a convertible?

Man: They have a daughter.

Daughter: *(comes over to window)* Where is she?

(Man points out the window and then moves away from the window.)

Daughter: I hate her already. Long, blonde hair, perfect teeth, stupid smile. She's probably a cheerleader and gets straight *A*'s. *(Daughter's mouth drops open. She pulls the imaginary blind open wider.)* Look at that car! It must be hers. Did you see the plate? *(reads it in a mocking tone)* 2RBB. I've had my license for a year with no car, and now 2RBB has to move in next door. I told you I hated her. *(pauses as she looks out the window)* Dad, there's your motorcycle! It's just like the one you want.

Man: *(rushes back to the window whining)* No!

Daughter: Even has the fringe on the seat.

Man: No!

(Man and Daughter also sit down. All three are angry and dejected.)

(Neighbor Man and Neighbor Woman enter as if coming to the front door. They carry a plate of cookies. The audience hears their whispered conversation; Man, Woman, and Daughter do not.)

Neighbor Woman: Look at that fountain. Our landscaping is nothing like this.

Neighbor Man: Well, we wanted to live in this neighborhood. It was the only house we could afford here.

Neighbor Woman: You don't need to mention that to them ... but I'm sure they figured it out. If they watched us unload our stuff, they probably thought the Beverly Hillbillies were moving in next door.

Neighbor Man: Why are we bringing cookies to them anyway? I thought the old neighbors were supposed to welcome the new ones.

Neighbor Woman: I just want to see what we're up against ... Look, the curtain's open. That's the table I want.

Neighbor Man: Look at her! A gorgeous home *and* a gorgeous wife to go with it.

(Everyone looks unhappy.)

Just Managing My Time

The monologue, "Just Managing My Time," addresses issues of work, workaholism, worship, rest, renewal, and honoring the Sabbath. A man who conducts business on his cell phone plugged into the wall of the men's restroom at church on Sunday has no problems with any of these things. He is just managing his time.

Cast
The monologue is delivered by a busy man. Everything he does is fast paced. He has no time to rest. He worships when it fits his schedule and his needs.

Setting And Costumes
There is no special set needed. All that is needed is a wall with an electrical outlet, or something that looks like an outlet that a cell phone charger can be plugged into. The man is dressed for church and business.

Props
Watch
Cell phone with a charger

(A man enters and dials a number on his cell phone. He puts it up to his ear, then takes it down and shakes his head. The battery is dead. He pulls the charger out of his pocket, plugs it into the wall and into his phone, and places his call. He waits for someone to pick up and looks impatiently at his watch. As he is talking he occasionally forgets he is plugged into the wall. He begins to walk around, accidentally unplugging the cord and getting very frustrated. He is waiting impatiently for someone to answer.)

Come on. Come on. *(now talking to Lance on the phone)* Lance, you're there. Great. I need the file you're working on by one o'clock.

(pauses as though listening to Lance) I know it's Sunday, which is the day before Monday, which is the day before Tuesday when I have to give the presentation. *(pauses)* Yes, I know it's Sunday morning. *(pauses)* I'm not at the office. I'm at church. *(pauses)* No, of course I'm not in the service talking on my phone. I'm in the men's bathroom. My battery's low. I had to plug in my charger. *(pauses)* I *am not* a workaholic. I'm just managing my time. *(pauses)* They're only singing in there, right now. I'll go in when the pastor starts talking, and by the time he's done my battery should be charged and I can finish calling my clients during the picnic. I'm going to the park with my family. Might as well get something done while I'm there. Hang on, Lance, I have another call.

(pushes a button to take the other call) Hello, this is Steve. *(pauses)* John, thanks for calling me back. *(pauses)* Yes, calm down. I'm fine. Have you set the meeting up for Wednesday? *(pauses and then with a little irritation)* Yes, that's what I called for. *(pauses)* Well, it seemed like an emergency to me. *(pauses)* Yes, I know it's Sunday. That only leaves three days until Wednesday. *(pauses)* Hey, I'm on the other line. Just give me a call when you get it set up, okay? 'Bye.

(pushes button to go back to other call) Lance, you still there? *(pauses)* Relax, there's a speaker here in the bathroom. I can hear what's going on. They're just doing the preliminaries: singing, praying, offering, that stuff. *(pauses)* What do you mean why do I bother? Our family goes to church together every week. You should try it sometime. *(pauses, then with a hint of self-righteousness)* Well, I guess everyone has priorities. Just make sure to get me the file by one. Bring it by the park so I can get started on it during the picnic. Hey, even better. I think there's a fax machine here at the church. I'll get the number and email it to you from my phone. Fax it by 12:50 and I can take it with me to the picnic.

(looks up as though listening to the speaker) Lance, gotta go. They're doing the handshaking thing. You won't believe this. I found out there's a guy here who works for Snider and Sons. He could really help us out. I need to go meet him. Hey, let me know if you and your family want to come to church with us. Remember, fax it by 12:50. *(pauses)* Okay. 'Bye. *(puts down phone to charge and rushes off to the service)*

Do You Know How Much It Hurts?

"Do You Know How Much It Hurts?" illustrates three styles of communication that are harmful to families: blowing up, stuffing feelings inside, and running away from feelings. Each member of this family deals with his or her feelings differently, but each is hurt because the feelings are never openly and honestly discussed. This drama can be used as a sermon starter for messages on communication, anger, honesty, speaking the truth in love, or related topics.

Cast
> Boss — no speaking lines
> Man — has a short temper
> Wife — is angry and hurt, but keeps her emotions inside — talks to her friend, but is very closed off
> Friend — woman who is a friend of the wife, caring, trying to help
> Daughter — young teenager, angry and hurt, and wants to get away

Setting And Costumes
> On stage is an empty table with two chairs. A radio sits nearby on a stand.
> Boss and Man are dressed in suits and each carries a briefcase. Woman, Friend, and Daughter are dressed casually.

Props
> Table with two chairs
> Radio
> Two briefcases
> Two coffee cups
> Cordless phone
> Suitcase and some clothes
> Teddy bear

Music
A song about family or running away or communication, whatever seems to fit.

(Man and Boss enter. Each carries a briefcase. They stand facing each other. Man has just been fired from his job. He rages while Boss listens and looks uncomfortable.)

Man: What do you mean you hope I understand? You hope I don't take it too hard? Did you just get fired from your job? No, you're the owner's son. You don't even have a real job to get fired from. Some of us have to work ... or did. Some of us have families and mortgages. Some of us have to eat. Did you think of that? *(waves a check in the air)* Do you think a measly check you call severance pay can make up for that? But at least it soothes your guilty conscience, doesn't it? You hire your friend, fire me, and then tell yourself you helped me out with this check. This is what I think of your stupid severance pay. *(He tears the check into several pieces and throws it in the air, picks up his briefcase, and stomps out. The Boss picks up his briefcase and walks out quietly.)*

(Wife and Friend enter carrying coffee cups. They sit at the table and face the audience.)

Wife: He's angry. When he feels hurt the whole neighborhood knows it. *(pauses)* I have a reason to be angry, too, you know.

Friend: Have you talked to him about it?

Wife: No. He's so angry about losing his job and whatever else happens to set him off. There's no good time to say, "We need to talk about our marriage."

Friend: That must feel bad.

26

Wife: Yeah, I guess it really hurts. Thanks for being concerned, but I don't need to talk to anyone about it really. The best thing to do is just go on ... keep it in. *(near tears)* Besides, there's so much in there that if I talk about any of it, I know the rest will come pouring out. There's no way I'm going to let that happen. That's how people's families fall apart. Keep it to yourself and be happy. That's my motto. *(shrugs)* It's worked so far. *(stands up and begins picking up the coffee cups and says without much feeling)* It's been good talking to you. *(both exit)*

(Daughter comes in talking on a cordless phone. She is carrying a suitcase with clothes draped over it and clothes stuffed under her arm as if she is in the process of hurriedly packing. She is speaking into the phone.)

Daughter: I am out of here. *(pauses)* I don't know, but I'll find somewhere. *(pauses)* What do you mean why not stay home? *(pauses)* You've been here with my parents. *(pauses)* They are too that bad. *(pauses)* My dad has this huge chip on his shoulder about everything. *(pauses)* Like what? Like my boyfriend's car made a drip of oil in the driveway, like I don't know what it means to work, like if his family weren't such a pain, he wouldn't be distracted at work and he'd still have a job. *(pauses)* My mom? No ... she doesn't say anything, just stuffs it all inside. Yeah, I'm waiting for her to explode. But I'm getting out of here before it happens. *(pauses)* Are you kidding? How could I stay? Do you know how much it hurts to live here? I have to get out. *(long pause)* Okay, I'll call you later. 'Bye.

(Daughter turns on the radio. Music begins to play. Music can be about running away, or family, or whatever seems to fit. As she listens to the music she is wiping her eyes and packing. She opens the suitcase and takes out a teddy bear, holds it to her for a moment, puts it back in the suitcase and then puts the clothes in. She closes the suitcase, takes a last look around and exits.)

Let Your Mind Dwell On These Things

Our minds dwell on and remember what our ears and eyes take in. This humorous monologue shows the struggle to dwell on whatever is pure while taking in whatever is not. It can be used with messages on becoming Christlike, scripture memorization, or choices in entertainment. It is based on Philippians 4:8.

Cast

A woman or man who is making some effort to memorize a scripture, but is unfocused and undisciplined.

Setting And Costumes

A table and chair are in the middle of the stage facing the audience. A radio and a closed Bible sit on the table.

No special costume is needed.

Props

Table and chair
Radio
Bible

(The woman [or man] sits behind a table facing the audience, speaking to herself/himself, trying to remember a verse.)

Whatever is ... Whatever is true ... or ... whatever is ... *(looks at audience)* I'm trying to memorize a verse. Maybe if I look it up. *(picks up Bible and talks to herself/himself, as she searches for the verse)* Philippians, Philippians, here it is. *(reading)* Philippians 4:8. What ever is true, whatever is honorable, whatever is right, whatever is pure, whatever is lovely, whatever is of good repute, if there is any excellence and if anything worthy of praise, let your mind dwell on these things.

Okay, I think I've got it. *(puts Bible down and tries reciting it again)* Whatever is lovely ... and um ... there's a good ... something ... a report maybe? *(makes a frustrated sound)* This is too hard. I can't remember it. *(tries again)* Whatever is good ... and, whatever ... Oh, whatever! *(The radio catches her attention. She starts to keep the beat to a rhythm as though the radio is on.)* I love this song. *(turns knob on radio as if turning it up and starts to sing. Make up a tune and rhythm. Sing loudly and off-key.)*

 I know, I know, I know I'm not your wife*
 But it'd be so right if you'd come see me tonight
 'Cause you know, you know, our love is so real
 I'd lie and kill and steal for you! *(the word "you" is very loud,*
   high pitched, and off-key)

I know all the words on this CD. I put it on repeat when I'm driving to work. *(starts singing again)*

 'Cause you know, you know, our love is so real
 I'd lie and kill and steal for you

(suddenly remembers the audience and stops singing) Oh. *(reaches to turn down the knob)* What was I doing? Learning this verse.

 Okay. *(reading)* Whatever is ... *(stops reading and looks up)* I think I have it now. I don't need to keep reading it. Whatever is ... good, whatever ... *(something across the room has caught her attention, stares as if looking at a television)* Whatever happened to the guy who played her boyfriend on this show? Remember? He got in a big fight with her husband, and the husband ended up in the hospital, then the boyfriend paid a doctor a lot of money to inject poison into his IV, and he almost died, then the boyfriend went to jail for drugs and the wife found out that she ... *(remembers she's trying to learn the verse)* Oh yeah, the verse.

 (reading) Whatever is true, whatever is honorable, whatever is right, whatever is pure, whatever is lovely, whatever is of good repute, if there is any excellence and if anything worthy of praise, let your mind dwell on these things. *(looks out at audience)* How am I ever going to learn this?

*If monologue is performed by a man change this line to "I know, I know, I know you're not my wife."

30

Just To Talk?

As with any sin, adultery begins with a few "innocent coincidences" and with lots of rationalization. This monologue exposes the thought processes and the small steps into sin that threaten to destroy a marriage and a life. This monologue can be used with a message on adultery, loneliness in marriage, or with a message about sin luring us away until it has destroyed us.

Cast
  Young woman

Props
  Telephone

(The young woman begins speaking slowly, as if reticent to talk about this.)

Don asked me to come over tonight ... just to talk and have some coffee. *(pauses)* I told him I'd call and let him know. His wife's out of town for the weekend, and ... my husband will be gone at school until at least eleven. *(with a hint of resentment)* Kyle's always gone until at least eleven. *(begins to dial then pushes button to end the call)*
  Neither of us said it, but we both know what will happen if I go over there tonight. Today when we saw each other during lunch, the attraction was so thick all we could do was sit there and try not to touch each other ... and that was in a crowded restaurant. Tonight, alone at his house, there will be nothing to stop us, and I'm not so sure I want to be stopped. *(suddenly sad and angry)*
  Marriage turned on me. I got married to share my love with Kyle, to have a life with him. Not only do we have nothing in common, we can't even have a simple conversation that doesn't

end in an argument: money, the house, sex, having kids, what we do on the weekends, even where we go to church. You name it; we argue about it. And of course he's always right. He's the law student. I'm just ... the receptionist who works to pay his tuition. *(sadly)* I've committed my *whole life* to someone I can't bear to be with. Now I've found someone I can't stay away from. *(begins to dial again)*

Why am I torturing myself over this? Don is a friend, just a good friend. There's been nothing physical between us. We're both adults. We can control ourselves. *(puts phone to ear to wait for an answer then quickly pushes button to end call and puts it down)* But we won't. I know we won't. All the emotions I've shut down over the years of marriage start to open back up when I'm with Don. And where my heart goes ... the rest of me wants to follow.

It didn't start this way. At first he was just the good-looking guy who made eye contact and smiled at me each time he got off the elevator by my desk. It felt good to be noticed. I started to think about him at night when I was going to bed alone. And then I started to think about him even when Kyle was at home, but emotionally somewhere else. I'd relive Don's eye contact that lasted long enough to mean something. At least I hoped it meant something. I wondered what he'd be like to talk to. When I felt ignored by Kyle, I'd imagine long conversations with Don that ... ended with a kiss.

Don usually left for lunch about 12:30 and went to the restaurant around the corner. I started arranging my schedule so I'd be walking to my car or the bank or lunch or somewhere at 12:30. We'd stop and talk for a minute. Don did some schedule arranging, too, and began showing up in the lobby just before my break. So we'd go get coffee. Just coincidences ... carefully planned coincidences.

It was easy to talk to him. So different than Kyle. I thought about him all the time. It got me through lonely nights at home and bad days at work. Our shared coffee breaks turned into long lunches, and soon I'd told him about the pain in my marriage ... and he told me about his. We talked about where we grew up, our families, old boyfriends and girlfriends, first dates, first kisses ...

and today at lunch he told me my husband must be crazy not to appreciate how beautiful and intelligent I am. He asked what I'd do if I wasn't married. I said this time I'd follow my heart. He said he would, too. Then we didn't know what to do except sit and look at each other ... and breathe a lot. When he walked me back to my desk he asked if I'd come over tonight for coffee ... just to talk. *(sighs and looks at phone)* Just to talk.

That's Just Too Weird

When life is uncertain, where do we turn? When we feel a void, how do we fill it? This sketch takes a humorous look at where we place our trust. It can be used as a sermon starter for messages dealing with anxiety, fear of the future, and the peace of God.

Cast
Instructor — vain woman who likes to sound like an expert
Students:
Partier — male or female, acts edgy and afraid until using the drugs in the bag, then is too relaxed
Money Lover — male or female
Christian — male or female

Setting And Costumes
Students sit in a semicircle around Instructor.
Instructor is dressed as though teaching a class. The students wear hooded shirts.

Props
Three chairs
Teaching notes
Five paper grocery bags — Three are carried by Instructor: The first bag holds a large makeup mirror and the other two bags can just be stuffed with paper to appear full. The Partier's bag contains some kind of alcohol in a can or bottle, something to smoke, drugs to take, and the like, the more the better. The purpose is to make it look exaggerated. The Money Lover's bag holds a wallet full of money.

(Students enter and take their seats — Partier and Money Lover are each carrying a paper grocery bag. Christian carries nothing. Instructor enters, carrying three paper grocery bags and teaching notes.)

Instructor: *(holds up teaching notes)* The purpose of this seminar is to help you deal with fear and anxiety and to send you out with confidence to face your future. Now, the way to have confidence is to know what you might encounter and prepare for it. Please take notes. This will be on the test. We'll begin with the ... less happy possibilities for your lives. *(begins to read very quickly and matter-of-factly from notes)* Terrorism is increasing. Germs are becoming more virulent, antibiotics less effective. There is global warming and we're due for a switch in magnetic poles any day. Meteors fly by the earth and our city is built on a fault line. On a more personal note, you will all likely live sixty or seventy more years. During that time you may face wars, crime, disease, deaths, divorce, drought, disaster, not to mention deep, deep disappointments, failed tests, flunked classes, lost jobs, and ... *(She stops suddenly as she notices Partier and Money Lover have slunk down into their chairs. They pull their hoods over their faces and wring their hands, looking terrified. Christian sits there calmly.)* I think that's enough for this session. Everyone take a deep breath and say, "I have nothing to fear but fear itself ... and lots of it."

Partier and Money Lover: *(each takes a deep breath)* I have nothing to fear but fear itself ... and lots of it.

Instructor: Very good. We'll take a higher power break. Take out the higher power you brought to class in a bag and commune with it. We'll start the next session in five minutes.

(Christian just sits and watches. Partier and Money Lover frantically open their bags. Partier begins to smoke, drink, and indulge in other addictive behaviors, with a great sense of relief. Money Lover gets the money out and counts it and breathes in its smell

36

with a great sense of relief. Instructor takes the mirror out of her bag and begins to worship herself in it. This goes on for a while, until Money Lover notices Christian is just sitting there.)

Money Lover: Didn't you bring anything?

Christian: I don't have a ... higher power bag.

Instructor: Don't worry. I have extras you can borrow. *(looks into one of her extra bags)* This one has a mirror, barbells, and a tanning light. You can get an amazing body. And this one *(looks in the other bag)* ... you'll like this one. This is the boyfriend bag. Well, the boyfriend's not in the bag, but his picture and phone number are. You should see him. He's gorgeous. I'd let him be my higher power any day.

Christian: No, thank you, I don't need a ... higher power bag.

Instructor: A higher power bag is required for this course. Besides, you'll never make it through life without one. When things get tough, you have to have something to turn to, otherwise you're sunk. *(speaks in her instructor voice again)* By the way class, in the next session we'll discuss all the ways you might sink: quicksand, sinkholes, depression, poverty, midlife crisis ... *(tries to hand a bag to Christian).*

Christian: I have God, so I don't need a higher power bag.

(The other three look at Christian.)

Money Lover: You said ... God?

Christian: Yes, I can face whatever is in my future because of God.

Instructor: And how do you intend to do that?

Christian: Instead of being anxious about anything, I just pray.

Partier: *(a little strung out by now, speaks slowly)* That's just *too* weird.

This Is My Life

God wants to do more in our lives than we can ask or imagine, but often we feel that because of the circumstances of our lives, the dreams we once had are impossible. In this drama a woman is encouraged to see her life through God's eyes. This drama works well for women's events such as retreats or luncheons.

Cast

Builder — woman in her twenties, thirties, or early forties; determined, but without dreams

Inquirer — woman who asks questions, makes an observation, and then goes on her way

Discourager — woman who tears down with her sugar-coated words

Friend — woman who enters a life and makes a difference

Setting And Costumes

No special setting or costumes are needed.

Props

25 large cardboard building blocks (shoeboxes wrapped in brown mailing paper work well)

(A woman is building her "life" with bricks or large blocks. She is placing them on the floor making a square of bricks around her, five on each side. She has three of the sides laid down so far. As she builds, she counts to make sure each side is just right.)

Builder: *(counting the bricks on each side)* One, two, three, four, five ... One, two, three, four, five ... One, two ...

Inquirer: *(enters and watches her, then interrupts the counting)* What are you building?

Builder: My life.

Inquirer: It's ... um ... well, a little small, isn't it?

Builder: It's cozy. Excuse me, *(moves Inquirer back a little)* you're standing right where my fourth wall goes.

Inquirer: How do you know all the dimensions of your life already? I mean ... you have so much of it ahead of you. *(begins walking around examining her "life")* You might want to expand over here. *(walks to another side)* Or do some planting over here. *(lifts up head and looks around in the distance)* Your property is amazing. There is so much for you here.

Builder: *(not listening to Inquirer, traces a little square beside the bricks with her toe)* And this ... *(finishes tracing)* will be my fence. *(turns back to count)* One, two, three, four, five. *(puts the last blocks in place and steps inside)* This is it. This is my life.

Inquirer: Are you sure? This is it?

Builder: *(steps out of square and begins walking around it's edges)* I have only a medium amount of education, *(turns corner)* less than medium finances, *(turns corner)* I'm a woman at home with three kids, *(turns corner)* and a husband, and a dog. I'd say my life is pretty well defined. *(steps back inside the square)* But thanks for asking.

Inquirer: Well, okay. Good-bye.

Builder: Good-bye. *(She goes back to silently counting and straightening the blocks and then sits back down. When Discourager begins to talk, Builder listens with a discouraged expression, but doesn't stop her.)*

Discourager: *(enters and examines the square — a little patronizing)* Oh, Honey ... five bricks? Are you sure you can handle a life that big? Here ... *(begins to rearrange making the square of bricks smaller and confining the Builder more and more)* Let's take a few out. I always say, "Don't dream big and you won't have big disappointments." Maybe if you'd finished your master's degree and had a little more money and time, you could handle a five-brick life. But you're young, and you have a family, and ... time goes so fast that soon you'll be old. How will you handle a five-brick life when you're eighty? Have you thought of that? No. I think a four-brick life is just perfect for you. *(finishes rearranging the bricks then decides to offer one last word of "encouragement")* You hang in there. You'll make it!

(Builder seems deflated, just nods and sits in her "life." Friend walks in gazing off into the distance. Walks right into the bricks knocking them out of place.)

Builder: *(annoyed, gets up, points at the scattered bricks)* You just walked into my life.

Friend: *(looks at the bricks)* Oh, you're right. Were you building it?

Builder: No, I finished building it. I was sitting in it.

Friend: I have to show you something.

(Builder doesn't want to leave her "life" but then hesitantly comes out and stands by Friend. Friend puts one arm around Builder's shoulder, with the other hand points out into the distance.)

Friend: Do you see that?

Builder: *(squinting, trying to see)* See what?

Friend: Keep looking.

Builder: What are we looking at?

Friend: Your life.

41

Builder: No, *(points toward bricks)* this is my life. I'd just finished building it when you walked into it.

Friend: *(motions out toward the distance)* But this is what God has for your life. *(continues to look, suddenly gets an expression as if she's seen something amazing)*

Builder: God knows I have three kids, a husband and...?

Friend: *(finishing her question)* And a dog? He knows.

Builder: He knows I didn't finish college?

Friend: He knows. He also knows that was one of your dreams. He knows all your dreams, the deepest desires of your heart. He planted them in you.

Builder: I've had to bury those dreams away. Do you know that I used to dream of a ten-brick life?

Friend: God dreams even more for you than a ten-brick life, more than you can imagine.

Builder: *(slightly anxious)* I ... wouldn't have enough bricks for all that. I only have enough for a five-brick life. And ... how would I ever manage a life like that? You know, I'm too young, and then soon I'll be too old, and what if ... *(falls silent for a moment)* Do you really think God wants to do all this in my life?

Friend: I do.

Builder: Well ... where do I start?

Friend: Start with these bricks. But build a pathway. I'll help you. And start with your dreams, but this time don't just bury them ... plant them.

(The two begin to build as the lights go out.)

Unsinkable

Can life be compartmentalized? If unfaithfulness leaks into one part of our life, will it sink us? This drama calls for four skilled actors whose lines weave together to tell the story of a man who has tried to compartmentalize his life just as the builder of the Titanic attempted to build separate unsinkable compartments in his ship. It is an emotional drama that will leave the audience moved and some of them shaken.

Cast

Four men. It is helpful if the four men are similar in appearance and build, but not at all necessary.

Unfaithful Man — delivers the lines that explain and justify the man's unfaithfulness to his family. He is trying hard to convince us he is in the right.

Family Man — delivers the lines telling the audience what a good family man he is. He tries to convince himself his unfaithfulness is a separate compartment of his life that does not affect his family.

Money Man — tells the audience how well he provided for his family

Praying Man — the only honest part of the man's compartmentalized life — shows us how the man's unfaithfulness has interfered with his prayer and has shipwrecked his life

Offstage Voice — minister

Offstage Voice — man (if prerecorded, use the voice of unfaithful man)

Setting And Costumes

No special setting is needed.

All four men are dressed exactly alike.

Props

Family picture, dollhouse, or picture of a house

Moneybag with a $ on the front

43

Additional Notes

At the end of the drama, as the last line is delivered and the lights go down, a picture projected on screens behind the actors showing the sinking *Titanic* or the *Titanic* as it was discovered on the ocean floor, is quite powerful.

(The four men enter. Two come from one side of the stage, two from another. They meet at the center of the stage and stand looking at one another as if they are looking into a mirror. They begin to fix their hair and adjust their clothing at the same time. As the wedding vows begin they turn to face the audience. The two men in the back step forward, so all four stand side by side. In front of Family Man sets something to represent a home and family, possibly a family picture or a dollhouse. In front of Money Man sets a moneybag with a $ on it. [Or the two men can hold the symbols of family and money.] The Praying Man bows his head.

As the men begin to talk they will finish each other's thoughts with no break in between to make it sound as though it is the speech of one person.

From offstage we hear a man taking his wedding vows. It may either be through an offstage microphone or prerecorded on tape or CD.)

Minister: *(offstage)* Do you take this woman to be your wife? Do you promise to love, honor, cherish, and protect her, forsaking all others and holding only unto her until death do you part?

Man: *(offstage)* I do.

Unfaithful Man: *(a little defensive)* And I did ... for eight years. But then I met the love of my life, the one I *should* have married. The problem was, of course ...

Family Man: *(a little guilty and worried)* I had a wife and two daughters.

Unfaithful Man: *(shrugs)* But it was time for my heart to move on. It could have torn me up; I'm a sensitive guy. It has ruined some men I know. Don't get me wrong. I'm a good person. I just had a little problem in my marriage.

Family Man: I supported my family well ...

Money Man: bought them everything they wanted.

Praying Man: *(lifts head)* I went to church. I even prayed sometimes. *(gets down on his knees and stays in that position until the end; shakes his head sadly)* But now I can't pray. I try, but ...

Unfaithful Man: *(abruptly)* I don't want to talk about that part. *(pauses)* I want you to understand: leaving my wife was my only option.

Family Man: It was better for her, too, I'm sure ... and for my daughters. I just wasn't happy there, and ... you know what it's like to live with an unhappy person.

Unfaithful Man: *(dreamily)* But when I'm with my new girlfriend, she makes me feel like *(throws his arms open)* I am the king of the world! *(puts arms back down as Praying Man says his next line)*

Praying Man: Except, I feel so far away from God.

Unfaithful Man: No, I can't start thinking about all that depressing stuff. That's how you sink. I read once about a ship builder. He had an interesting theory. Build the ship with separate, unsinkable compartments. If one section took on water, the rest could still float. I bet not even *God* could sink a ship like that. I don't know if the guy ever built it; I didn't finish reading the article. But it's a great metaphor for life.

Praying Man: I wish I could talk to God. I feel like *I'm* sinking.

Unfaithful Man: I've got to stop thinking that. I need to think like the shipbuilder. I can't let this one little marital problem affect the rest of my life.

Family Man: Yes, I've left my wife and family,

Unfaithful Man: but that's only one piece of my life. It doesn't have to affect the rest of it.

Family Man: They'll get over it; they're strong. Maybe they'll even be happier, and ...

Money Man: financially I'm fine. I can afford alimony if I need to. I can even buy my children extra presents now and then, and my job's going well. At work I can block out all this family stuff and just focus on getting things done.

Praying Man: But I can't pray. There's something blocking my prayers. It feels like there is ice in my heart where it used to be warm. I'm sinking and it's so dark.

Unfaithful Man: But when I'm with Jennifer, I'm the king of the world. I love her. I know we were meant to be together. It just happened at an inconvenient time.

(Pause)

Family Man: Tomorrow is Jordan's fourth birthday. She said the only thing she wanted was for Daddy to be home again. Maybe Jennifer and I can pick her up and take her to the zoo. I think she'd like Jennifer.

Unfaithful Man: *(excitedly)* I sure do! You know, I think I can do this.

Family Man: I can be a dad, and ...

Unfaithful Man: I can have a girlfriend, and ...

Money Man: I can do great at work, and ...

Unfaithful Man: I'll even go find a new church. Maybe I can't pray right now, but that's not a big deal. It's probably normal. I've had a lot of changes this year.

Family Man: I don't have to let a little problem with my wife mess up my whole life. I'm a good guy. A good dad. I ... *(confidently lying to himself)* I was even a good husband.

Money Man: A good worker. A good employer.

Unfaithful Man: And with Jennifer ... I'm the king of ...

Praying Man: *(interrupts)* My heart's almost frozen now.

Unfaithful Man: *(looks over at Praying Man alarmed then back at audience)* But I'm fine. I'm ... I'm just fine.

Family Man: *(desperate)* I'm a good father.

Money Man: *(louder and more desperate)* I'm a success at work.

Unfaithful Man: *(even louder as though trying to convince)* I am the king of the world.

(Pause)

Praying Man: *(quietly, but with grief)* I'm going down.

All Men: *(together)* I'm sinking. *(they lower their heads into their hands)*

(The lights go down.)

A Problem With Your Card

Is life to be spent collecting debt and then trying to manage it? This couple begins to wonder as they find themselves deep in debt with seemingly no way out. This drama deals with attitudes toward spending and the way we try to hide our financial problems. It works well as an introduction to messages on finances and as an introduction to classes on financial management.

Cast

Man — embarrassed at his problem in the restaurant and becoming increasingly concerned over the state of their finances

Woman — not quite as concerned as her husband, but anxious to get out of the restaurant at the end of the sketch

Server — friendly and helpful, becomes embarrassed for the couple as their credit cards continue to be turned down

Setting And Costumes

The scene takes place in a restaurant.

The man and woman are dressed up to indicate the dinner might have been an expensive one.

Props

Small table with tablecloth and candle
Two cups and saucers
Meal check
Credit card folder used in restaurants
Man's wallet with at least three credit cards
Checkbook
Woman's purse and wallet
Cell phone

(Man and Woman sit together at a table in a restaurant finishing their coffee after a big meal. Server enters to check on them and bring the bill.)

Server: How was your meal?

Woman: Wonderful.

Man: Very good. Thank you.

Server: Can I bring you anything else this evening?

Woman: No, thank you.

Man: Everything was great.

Server: Here's your check. I'll take care of it for you when you're ready.

Man: *(takes check)* Thank you.

(Server exits. Man takes out his wallet, pulls out a credit card and begins to place it in the folder.)

Woman: That card's over its limit. I tried to use it at the mall today. Use the VISA instead.

Man: *(takes out another card and places it with the check)* What did you buy at the mall? *(tone is just curious, not accusatory)*

Woman: New drapes and blinds for the living room.

Server: *(enters, picks up the check)* I'll be right back. *(exits)*

Man: *(to Server)* Thanks. *(to Woman)* Didn't you buy drapes last month?

Woman: Yes, but I got tired of them. These will make the room so much brighter.

Man: Did you happen to see that plasma TV while you were there?

Woman: *(excitedly)* Oh, I meant to tell you. It's on sale now, and you don't have to make a payment for six months.

Man: Good, that will give us time to figure out how to pay for it. If we get it tomorrow, I can watch the game on it Saturday.

Server: *(enters, hands back credit card)* I'm sorry, Sir, there's a problem with your card.

Man: *(embarrassed)* Oh ... yeah. *(fumbles through his wallet)* Here, I'll put it on this one.

Server: Thank you. I'll be right back.

Woman: What's the problem with our VISA card?

Man: *(hesitates)* Golf clubs.

Woman: Well ... I guess you needed them.

Man: *(sheepish)* I did.

Woman: Hey, don't be embarrassed about the credit card. This kind of thing happens to everyone.

Man: It just seems to be happening to us a lot lately.

Server: *(enters and hands back this card also)* I'm sorry. This card wasn't approved either.

Man: *(very embarrassed and flustered)* Oh, yes ... I should have remembered that. *(looks through wallet)* Here. Try this one.

(Server takes the card and exits.)

Woman: *(when Server is gone)* Will that one work?

Man: I don't know ... We have so many I've lost track. Do you have any cash in case it doesn't work?

Woman: *(pulls out wallet and opens it)* Three dollars ... and ... eighteen cents.

Man: Well, that might cover the croutons. I don't have cash either. The ATM wouldn't give me any. Our account is overdrawn.

Woman: You should have taken it out of savings.

(Man just sits looking at her and shakes his head.)

Woman: Our savings is gone?

Man: The boat. Remember?

Server: *(enters with no credit card)* I'm really sorry. That one wouldn't work either, and the credit card company asked us to hold on to it.

Man: If you can come back in just a minute, I'll have it for you.

Server: Certainly.

Man: *(as an afterthought to the Server as she is exiting)* Do you still take checks?

Server: *(returns to the table)* We had to stop taking them. Too many were bouncing. *(noticing their distress)* But I'll see if we can make an exception for you. *(exits)*

Man: Thank you. *(takes out a checkbook)*

Wife: We can't cover it.

Man: I know. We'll figure it out in the morning. I just want to get out of here. This is embarrassing. *(pauses)* Do you ever feel like we're sinking?

Woman: Sinking?

Man: You know, like we're too deep in debt and trying to bail ourselves out with credit cards?

Woman: It's just life. Most of life is spent juggling your debts.

Man: And then what?

Woman: I don't know ... And then you die and leave them for someone else to juggle? *(shrugs shoulders)*

Man: Or you can't pay your bill in a restaurant and you die of embarrassment. *(looks down at the checkbook)* Here's that tithe check.

Woman: The one we were waiting on to make sure we didn't need the money for something else?

Man: Yes.

Woman: I guess we better not put it in this week, either.

Server: *(enters, very embarrassed for them)* I'm sorry. My manager says we can't accept your check. Your name is on a ... a list.

Woman: A list?

Server: A list of people with returned checks.

Woman: Can we have another minute?

Server: Of course. *(exits)*

(Woman pulls out a cell phone begins to dial.)

Man: What are you doing?

Woman: Gene and Mandy only live a mile from here. Maybe they can help us out.

Man: *(getting irritated)* We can't tell anyone about this.

Woman: *(also irritated)* What do you propose?

Man: I don't know. We'll think of something ... but we're not calling anyone. You just don't tell people you're having money problems ... especially people at church. We'll figure it out ... ourselves.

(Man and Woman both rest their heads in hands and look down. Lights down.)

The Voice Of Despair

Each of us long for a purpose and a meaning to life. We find it in God, but all too often we look to everyone and everything else. This drama illustrates the ways we try to find meaning in life apart from God and the ways we are told our lives are pointless.

Cast

Man — really hoping there is some purpose to his life, but doubts there is

Voice Of Despair — (male voice offstage) represents the accusations of Satan as well as the messages from society that our lives have no purpose except the ones we give them

Salesperson — (woman) animated and shallow

Career Man — (man) has a plan and is in a hurry

Drunk — (man) a little obnoxious and clearly drunk

Woman — subtly seductive (should be seductive in voice rather than in actions or in dress)

Setting And Costumes

The stage is empty except for a large sign that reads "YOU ARE HERE." An arrow on the sign points down.

Man is dressed in slacks, a dress shirt, and tie. Salesperson is dressed in a skirt and jacket. Career Man is dressed in a suit. Drunk is disheveled. Woman is dressed to appear attractive and draw attention to herself, but is not dressed immodestly.

Props

Sign that reads, "YOU ARE HERE" with an arrow pointing down

Spray bottle of cologne

Large gold watch that can be quickly put on

Set of keys

Small shopping bag gift bag

Briefcase

Ladder
Cell phone
Two bottles or cans that appear to be some type of alcohol

(Man enters, stands in front of the sign to read it and then begins his conversation with Voice Of Despair. As he talks he looks out just above the eye level of the audience.)

Man: *(looks up at sign and then says to himself)* I'm here all right, but what am I here *for?*

Voice Of Despair: You *shouldn't* be here. *You* were an accident.

Man: *(looks around a little startled to hear the voice, but decides to have a conversation)* I was hoping maybe there was a reason, a purpose.

Voice Of Despair: You're one insignificant person out of billions. How could you have a purpose? Who would give you a purpose anyway?

Man: God?

Voice Of Despair: *(laughs)* God? Let me tell you something. There's random chance, and there's your own hard work. You take what you get and you work like crazy to make it better ... *(with resignation)* or you don't. And then you die.

Man: That's it?

Voice Of Despair: That's it.

Man: So what do I do?

Voice Of Despair: Don't ask me. Just do what everyone else does.

Man: *(with despair and resignation)* Okay.

Salesperson: *(Enters carrying a small shopping bag containing a bottle of cologne, a watch, and a set of keys. She carries a suit jacket over her arm. She sprays a sample of cologne on the Man's arm and talks in an animated voice.)* You were born to shop. *(puts the jacket on him, puts the watch on his arm, and hands him the set of keys)* The one who dies with the most toys wins. *(exits)*

(Man looks at what has just been given him. Looks puzzled, but then pleased.)

Career Man: *(Enters. He is in a hurry, carrying a briefcase and a ladder. He sets up ladder, puts down briefcase, and shakes Man's hand.)* Your resume looks great!

Man: *(pleased)* Thank you.

(As they shake hands the Career Man's cell phone rings.)

Career Man: Excuse me. *(answers phone)* Yes. *(pauses)* I'll have it for you first thing in the morning. *(pauses)* I'll ... have it for you tonight then. *(quickly puts phone away and hands Man the briefcase)* Here, take this. *(takes Man's arms and quickly walks him to the ladder)* Hurry, if you start climbing now, you can reach the top before you retire. Now hurry ... and good luck. *(exits)*

(Man begins climbing.)

Drunk: *(stumbles in carrying two drinks and walks to ladder)* Hey, where you going in such a hurry? Relax! Come down here. Have another drink.

Man: No. I've got to keep working. I already had a drink this morning to help me climb this thing.

Drunk: Oh, come on. You only go around once, you know. You've got to live a little.

(Man climbs down from the ladder and takes a drink from him. At first, Man is hesitant, but quickly warms up to the idea. They sit down beside the ladder. Drunk remains by the ladder until the end.)

Woman: *(walks by and talks in a seductive voice to Man)* I have what *you* need. *(exits)*

Man: *(shrugs, stands up and takes a few steps to follow Woman, then stops and looks around at Drunk and the ladder and shakes his head)* I was really hoping there was something more.

The Voice Of Purpose

The man in the drama has found a relationship with God, and the Voice of Despair has lost his power to discourage him or cause hopelessness. The man is writing for himself a record of what God has done. This drama introduces the idea of recording in writing what God has done as a remembrance of his faithfulness. This drama can be used to follow up a retreat or time of spiritual growth in a church.

Cast

Man —man who is confident of who he is in Christ (should be the same actor used in "The Voice of Despair")

Voice Of Despair — male voice offstage that represents the accusations of Satan as well as the messages from society that our lives have no meaning other than the ones we give them (should be the same actor used in "The Voice of Despair")

Setting And Costumes

The setting is the man's home, possibly a garden or patio. Any type of chair, lawn chair, or chair with table to suggest the man is at home will work.

Man is dressed casually.

Props

Chair
Journal
Pen

_____

(Man sits writing in a journal. He is seated in a chair or at a table. Voice Of Despair is heard, but the character is never seen.)

Voice Of Despair: Oh, it's you, the accident, the mistake, *(laughs cruelly)* the one who's looking for his purpose. So, did you find it? *(laughs, then stops suddenly when the man answers, "Yes")*

Man: *(looks up from his writing)* Yes. I am God's, his workmanship, created in Christ Jesus to do good works, which God has prepared for me to do. I have an extraordinary purpose.

Voice Of Despair: *(sarcastically)* Oh, so now you go to church on Sunday morning. You do your religious duty once a week. Some purpose.

Man: No. I'm not talking about duty. I'm talking about love.

Voice Of Despair: *(flatly)* Love?

Man: I love the Lord my God with all my heart and with all my soul and with all my mind and with all my strength.

Voice Of Despair: Sounds pretty *all*-encompassing. So what's left over for *you*?

Man: A personal relationship with the Creator of the universe.

Voice Of Despair: *(trying to sound bored, but is desperate to get out of there)* Oh, yeah, that. Well, I've got to run.

Man: Yes, you do. *(goes back to writing for a moment, then looks up and begins to speak to audience)*
    That was the Voice Of Despair. I imagine he's visited you. too. I used to believe his accusations. I believed I had no purpose. I believed I was so insignificant that it didn't matter how I lived. Everywhere I turned were doubts, accusations, questions with no answers. Everywhere I turned there was hopelessness. *(pauses, and then continues with a smile)*
    I remember when I was little ... I was afraid there were monsters in my closet. I'd call out to my father and he would come in

and turn on the light. The monsters would be gone. Well I've been calling out to my Heavenly Father, and he has stepped in and turned on the light. All my fears about my life having no purpose are gone. You see, I've been asking God to change my heart, to live in my mind, to introduce me to his family, and teach me how to love them. And he has! *(He holds up what he's been writing on.)* That's what I'm writing: a remembrance, a memorial of what God has done for me. Because I know that Voice Of Despair will try to talk to me again, but I can say, "God met me. God of all creation met with *me* and I am changed. I have a purpose!"

Before this, I spent years trying to figure out the meaning of life on my own. I ended up tangled in knots of confusion and destruction and self-absorption. The only *real* thing I discovered is, there is no meaning without God. *(with a sense of awe and wonder)* But with him ... With him life is full; it's rich and meaningful. It's like the life of an outcast who finds he is the son of the king. It's like shuffling through a dusty, old field and discovering a treasure. It's like looking into the sunrise and finding a color you never knew existed. It's ... as you can tell, beyond my ability to describe. It's something to be lived, and it's something to be recorded and remembered. *(pauses)* It's the place God and I begin our journey. *(continues writing)*

Disconnected

Christ says that without him we can do nothing. When we attempt life under our own power, we end up running in circles. This man's frustrating woodworking experience is a humorous picture of our own lives when we are disconnected from God's power.

Cast

Disconnected Man — a few disconnections within himself allow him to avoid and deny the real reason for his lack of power

Setting And Costumes

The stage is rather dimly lit. The scene takes place in a garage. The man is dressed to work in his garage.

Props

Two small tables
Books
Trouble light
Drill box containing new drill, instruction manual, and drill bits
Piece of wood

———————

(Two small tables sit on the stage. On one table sits a jumble of books and a trouble light. The cord is unplugged and dangles over the edge of the table in view of the audience. On the other table is a drill box and a piece of wood that is being made into a shelf. When the lights come up, a man is standing by the table with the drill box, calling offstage as if answering his son.)

I'm out here in the garage. I'm drilling the holes in the shelf for Mom's cabinet. *(pauses to listen)* Yes, you can go camping with Kevin and his dad. *(pauses)* No, we don't have any batteries for the flashlight. Just use it without batteries this time. We'll get some later. Have a good time.

(picks up drill box and begins to read in an awed voice) Three-eighths inch drive, variable speed, lock-on trigger mechanism. *(He carefully takes it out of the box, holds it up as if inspecting a gun, puts in a drill bit, blows on the end of it like he's cooling a smoking gun, puts it to the wood and squeezes the trigger. When nothing happens, he holds it up to look at it and squeezes the trigger again.)* Just my luck. I got the three-eighths inch drive, variable speed, lock-on trigger mechanism deluxe drill ... that doesn't drill. Let's see if there's a manual in here. *(takes manual out of box, opens it, and reads)* One: make sure the drill is connected to a 120-volt power outlet. *(looks disgusted and tosses the manual aside)* Who writes these things? They are so dry.

(picks up drill and looks at it again) I had another book. Where is it? *(takes the drill with him dragging the cord behind him; walks to the table with the books, sits the drill down, and digs through the books)* Here it is: *The Do It Yourselfer's Book of Doing It Yourself. (opens book to the back, squints, holds the book up and at different angles to try to get some light)* It's getting dark in here. *(walks to the lamp and turns it one click, then tries to read again but continues to move the book around and stumble over all the words)* Troubleshooting ... page 38. *(turns pages)* Or maybe 83 *(turns the lamp another click and flips more page)* Or maybe not. *(thumbs through the book)* Here's something in big letters. *(struggles to see the words)* If your drill ... If your drill doesn't work ... try harder, and remember ... you have ... the powder? No ... the power. You have the power to make your drill work. *(repeats to understand it)* If your drill doesn't work, try harder, and remember you have the power to make your drill work. *(shuts the book, sets it down and picks up drill, and says confidently)* I can do this.

(puts the drill to the wood and squeezes the trigger — nothing) I have the power to make my drill work. *(He puts the drill to the wood and begins circling the table while holding the drill on the wood. He does this a few times before getting tired and stopping.)* I guess it's a manual-power drill. *(picks up the cord)* This

cord really gets in the way. I should have bought a cordless one. *(looks at his work)* So far ... I've made one small dent. *(takes a deep breath)* I can do this. *I* have the power to make my drill work. *(He holds the drill on the wood and circles the table as quickly as he can, finally stops, exhausted, and sits down on the floor with his drill. He's made a new discovery and he's not happy about it.)*

I don't think this drill works. I'm wasting my time out here in the garage with a broken drill. Well, my wife can just forget about her shelf. My son can forget about me making that desk, and my neighbor's not getting my help putting his workbench together. *(disillusioned)* You can send messages by computer, you can watch movies off those little disks, you can microwave your food ... At least they say you can do all those things. I can never get any of them to work ... With all that technology you'd think someone could make a power drill that works. *(disgusted)* I'm through with woodworking. *(gets up and lays drill on table with cord hanging down in front)* I'm going to watch television. I hope *it* works. *(clicks "off" the light and exits)*

(The stage lights stay up a few seconds after he exits so the audience can look at the disconnections.)

Pass The Cheerios

Can we keep our passion for life? Can growing older mean growing in joy, or like this couple, does it have to mean that our joy runs out? We watch these two grow up, get married, have a family, grow old, and then grow bored. Does it have to be that way, or can joy follow us through life?

Cast

He — man of any age, who appears to be of similar age to the female character (through quick changes of costumes, he will play the parts of a child, a young man, and an old man)

She — woman of any age, who appears to be of similar age to the male character (through quick changes of costumes, she will play the parts of a child, a young woman, and an old woman)

Setting And Costumes

No special setting is needed.

Both characters dress in neutral colors. Through the use of various hats and jackets they age. For example, large children's hats or funny headbands for the characters as children, school letter jackets to show them as teenagers, a wedding veil and jacket at their wedding, a suit coat for him and pillow for her to show him busy working and her as pregnant, a shawl and scarf for her, a hat for him to show them in their older years.

Props

Table

Box of Cheerios

Several containers of Play-doh and a Play-doh toy that makes "spaghetti"

Skateboard

Phone

Bouquet of pink flowers

Two cereal bowls

Two spoons

Additional Notes

To help with the flow of this drama, short segments of instrumental or vocal music between the scenes allow the characters time to make costume changes and smoothly transition to the next scene.

———————————

(He and She are dressed as, and are acting like five-year-olds. They sit side-by-side at a table playing with Play-doh. A box of Cheerios sits on the table. She has made a Play-doh turtle. He is squeezing the Play-doh through a Play-doh toy to make spaghetti. He picks up the spaghetti holds it up and drops it back down on the table several times.)

He: Look, spaghetti. *(picks it up and drops it again)*

She: *(giggles and puts her turtle in the spaghetti)* My turtle's eating your spaghetti.

He: *(laughing)* Turtles don't eat spaghetti.

She: It's a spaghetti turtle.

He: Spaghetti turtle? *(puts spaghetti on her turtle, starts saying in a singsong voice)* Spaghetti turtle, spaghetti turtle.

She: *(joins him; both sing)* Spaghetti turtle, spaghetti turtle.

He: *(quickly smashes some of the spaghetti into turtle shape and pours out a pile of cheerios from the box.)* I made a Cheerio turtle. *(makes munching sounds as he pretends his turtle is eating the Cheerios)*

She: *(talking to turtle)* Hey, turtle, I like Cheerios, too.

He: Me, too.

(They both make munching sounds as they eat Cheerios.)

She: Want to come to my house and see my new puppy?

He: I'll ask my mom. *(gets up from table and leaves the Cheerios and Play-doh there)* Come on.

(She gets up to follow him.)

He: Can I feed your puppy?

She: Sure.

He: *(calling as they exit)* Mom, can I go to Brooke's house?

She: *(heard offstage)* Look, it's raining! Try to catch some. *(begins to sing)* It's raining. It's pouring. The old man is snoring.

He: *(joins her)* ... The old man is snoring.

* * *

(He and She enter dressed as teenagers. Their conversation takes place away from the table with the Play-doh and the Cheerios. He enters on his skateboard. She enters from the other side. Both are a little self-conscious in the other's presence.)

She: Hi.

He: Oh, hi, Brooke.

She: What are you doing?

He: *(acting cool)* Just hanging out. How about you?

She: I have to go home to feed and walk the dog.

He: Oh, hey, watch this. *(does something on skateboard)*

She: Cool.

He: Are you going to the game tonight?

She: Yeah. Are you?

He: Yeah. I'll look for you.

She: *(happy)* Okay. 'Bye.

He: 'Bye.

(She exits. He does something on his skateboard to try to impress her and exits.)

*   *   *

(He and She are dressed for their wedding. They enter together.)

She: Can you believe this is our wedding? We're getting married.

He: Remember when we were little and we used to make our Play-doh turtles eat Cheerios?

She: *(laughing)* Yes. *(dreamily)* I hope our kids are just like you.

He: Will you still love me when I'm a little old man?

She: Of course. You won't ever get tired of me?

He: Never.

(They look dreamily at each other and exit arm in arm.)

*   *   *

(He is now a young adult. He rushes in very excited. He is on the phone and carries a bouquet of pink flowers.)

He: Dad, Mom, it's me. It's a girl! *(pauses)* Seven pounds, nine ounces. *(pauses)* Jennifer Lynn. *(pauses)* Brooke's doing great. She's really tired, but she's so happy. You should see her. *(pauses)* Okay. I'll tell her. How's the dog? *(pauses)* Thanks for taking care of him. *(pauses)* 'Bye. *(exits)*

* * *

(He enters, again on the phone. He is still a young adult, but a more tired one. He is happy, but a little less enthusiastic.)

He: *(voice sounds as if talking to a young child)* Hi, Jennifer. This is Daddy. Guess what. *(pauses)* You're a big sister now. *(pauses)* No, a brother: Andrew. *(pauses)* Brothers are nice, too. Do you want to come see him later? *(pauses)* Okay. I'll come get you pretty soon. Can I talk to Grandma again? *(pauses)* 'Bye. I love you. *(pauses)* Hi, Mom. *(pauses then continues, concerned)* Mom? *(pauses)* It's okay. *(sadly)* I wish Dad could see Andrew, too. I'll be there as soon as I can to pick up Jennifer. *(pauses)* 'Bye. *(exits)*

* * *

(He and She enter. She is very pregnant. She is cleaning the Play-doh off the table putting it back into the container and picking up Cheerios off the floor.)

She: This is such a mess. *(bends down with much effort to pick up a Cheerio)* I am so tired of picking up Cheerios. *(picks up the Play-doh container and looks at it with tired annoyance)* Who thought of this stuff anyway?

He: I'll let the dog in to eat the Cheerios off the floor.

71

She: *(looks at him a little annoyed at his "helpful suggestion")* He sheds too much. *(sits down)* I'm so tired.

He: *(sits down too)* Me, too. We always wanted three kids.

She: I still do. I'm just ... so tired. I have to take Andrew for his check-up. Can you drop Jennifer off at school? I don't want her to walk in the rain.

He: Sure.

(They tiredly exit in different directions. She takes away the Play-doh and leaves the Cheerios box on the table.)

* * *

(He and She are now old. They enter carrying cereal bowls and spoons. They sit at the table again side-by-side. Their lines are delivered with little emotion.)

She: *(picks up the Cheerios box and pours the last of it into her bowl and looks into the box to make sure it's really empty)* Did you put the garbage out? It's Friday.

He: It's not Friday. It's Thursday.

She: It's Friday. The cereal just ran out. It always runs out on Friday.

He: It's only Thursday. I ate a few extra bowls last night. I couldn't sleep.

She: Was your back hurting?

He: Yeah.

(Quiet for a moment.)

She: Do you want to go the store today for more cereal?

He: No. It's going to rain.

She: Oh. *(pauses)* How do you know?

He: I watched the Weather Channel for three hours last night.

She: Oh.

(A long silence)

He: It's really quiet around here.

She: We could get a dog.

He: It would just get old.

She: Yeah.

He: *(looks at his empty bowl)* Are you sure the Cheerios are gone?

She: They're gone.

Flowers On A Saturday

"Flowers On A Saturday" is the story of gossip. It illustrates the breaches in relationships that rumors, speculations, and careless conversations can cause.

Cast
Jim — young fiancé of Jennifer — Jim is the one being gossiped about
Dave — man of any age
Steven — Sandy's husband
Sandy — Steven's wife
Jennifer — young woman — Jim's fiancée

Setting And Costumes
No set is needed, however, outdoor patio furniture, potted plants, and such may be placed around the stage to give the feeling of front yards.
All actors wear casual, Saturday morning clothes.

Props
Large bouquet of flowers
Newspaper
Bag of groceries

(Jim enters the stage carrying a newspaper and large bouquet of flowers. He is enjoying the morning, smelling the flowers, glancing at the headlines of the newspaper as he walks across the stage. He meets his neighbor, Dave, who is walking toward him.)

Jim: Good morning, Dave.

Dave: Good morning.

Jim: Beautiful day.

Dave: *(nods)* Nice flowers.

Jim: I'm going to see Jennifer. Thought they'd make a nice surprise.

(They walk off in different directions.)

Jim: *(calls)* Talk to you later.

Dave: 'Bye.

(Jim exits. Dave continues walking across stage. Steven enters carrying a bag of groceries and almost runs into Dave.)

Steven: Oh, hi. I didn't see you.

Dave: Did you see Jim? It looked like he just left the store, too.

Steven: *(shakes head)* Didn't see him.

Dave: He had a fight with Jennifer. A bad one.

Steven: You mean his fiancée?

Dave: Yep.

Steven: Did he tell you that?

Dave: No.

Steven: Did you hear them fighting?

Dave: No.

Steven: Did someone else tell you about it?

Dave: No.

Steven: Well then how do you know? Did he have a black eye or something?

Dave: No. *(pauses to make his announcement more grand)* He brought her flowers this morning.

Steven: *(he understands the importance of this announcement)* Oh! Flowers? Really? You sure it's not her birthday or something like that?

Dave: Nope.

Steven: Must be in big trouble. I wonder what he did?

Dave: They're probably fighting about his new secretary. I heard she's not real bad looking.

Dave and Steven: Hmmmmm.

Steven: Well, I've gotta go. See you later.

Dave: See ya.

(Dave exits. Steven continues walking across the stage and sees his wife who has just entered the stage.)

Steven: Oh, hi, honey. I've got the groceries. Sandy, have you talked to Jennifer lately? I'm kind of worried about her. Jim's been seeing way too much of his secretary. I'm afraid it might break up his engagement with Jennifer.

Sandy: *(surprised)* Jim and Jennifer? I just saw Jim. He's always so sweet to Jennifer. He was bringing her flowers. On a Saturday morning! That's romantic.

Steven: He's just trying to get himself out of trouble. *(sarcastically)* How romantic.

Sandy: I'll talk to her.

(Steven exits. Sandy continues walking and finds Jennifer as she enters the stage. Jennifer is holding the flowers, smiling and smelling them.)

Sandy: Jennifer, I just want you to know if you need someone to talk to, you can come to me.

Jennifer: *(puzzled)* Thank you.

Sandy: I'd never suspect this stuff of Jim. I thought it was so romantic that he'd bring you flowers on a Saturday morning. Steven only brought me flowers once — the day after he forgot our anniversary. But then I heard everyone talking about your problems and that Jim's been dating his secretary. I guess you never know. Anyway, I am really sorry. And remember, if you need anyone to talk to....

(Sandy exits. Jennifer looks at the flowers and lowers them so she now holds them down by her side. She goes to find Jim. Jim enters and greets her with a big smile. Jennifer throws the flowers by his feet and looks angry. Jim throws up his hands in confusion.)

Grace

God's grace finds us wherever we are. It found Beth at the end of a marriage and on the edge of death. It found Rhonda at the park on the edge of despair. This drama can be used as an introduction to a message on God's grace or to demonstrate how God uses our past pain to minister to others.

Cast

Two women in their twenties, thirties, or early forties.

Rhonda has come through some tough times, but now has the peace and strength to reach out to Beth.

Beth is frustrated and a little hardened by life. Her anger with her ex-husband causes her to tell her story to a stranger at a park.

Setting And Costumes

The setting is a park. A bench sits in the center of the stage. Trees and flowers may be placed on stage, if desired.

Rhonda is dressed for a day at the park. Beth is dressed for a day at work.

Props

Large sand bucket with shovels and sand toy
Beach bag or small food cooler

Rhonda: *(Enters carrying a sand bucket, sand toys, and beach bag or food cooler. She sits on the bench and calls out as though talking to her young daughter playing at the park.)* You're doing great on that swing, Rachel.

Beth: *(Enters, frustrated. She sits on the bench and calls out to her daughter.)* Get out of the dirt! I have to take you to your dad's in an hour. *(pauses)* No, I didn't bring any snacks. We'll get some on the way after we leave the park.

Rhonda: I have an extra orange. Would she like it?

Beth: No. She's fine. *(pauses as if listening impatiently to her daughter, then calls out to her)* Yes, you are fine. Just play on the swings and stay out of the water. *(to Rhonda)* Every time I take her to her dad's, he complains to me as soon as we walk through the door. *(mimicking)* "She's a mess, and that's the dress I bought her. It wasn't cheap, you know."

Rhonda: *(quiet for a moment as she is wondering how to respond)* Do you share custody?

Beth: *(an angry laugh)* That's what the judge calls it. I call it something else. But you probably wouldn't want to hear it. I get her every other weekend. He gets her the rest of the time. *(with deep sarcasm)* He can offer her a more stable environment. A better house ... and a *(spits out word)* stepmother who doesn't have to work and can spend time with her. *(angry and on the verge of tears)*

Rhonda: What's your daughter's name?

Beth: Grace. We ... I call her Gracie.

Rhonda: How did you decide to name her Grace?

Beth: Her heart stopped just before she was born. And ... *(remembering and realizing)* and I told God if he would bring her back to me I'd start going to church and get my life together. We had another name picked out, but when the doctors got her heart started, all I could think of was the word, "grace."

Rhonda: What did her father think about naming her Grace?

Beth: *(laughing again)* He said it was weak. He said in the real world there was no such thing as grace. But I insisted, so he gave in and we named her Grace.

Rhonda: I don't think Grace is weak at all.

Beth: Why?

Rhonda: It's a beautiful name; God's grace is the only reason I'm alive and have my daughter.

Beth: *(studies her and then looks down at Rhonda's wedding ring)* Well, you appear to be married still. Are you married to her dad?

Rhonda: Yes ... *(deciding whether to delve into her own difficult past)* We married last year ... for the second time. Two months before Rachel was born, he left me. We were divorced for three years. A week after he left me I attempted suicide. It was only because of God's grace that Rachel and I lived.

Beth: *(suddenly identifies with Rhonda's story)* Were you glad you lived?

Rhonda: No, not at first. I was angry. I remember screaming at God.

Beth: I'd be afraid to scream at God. I already have my ex on my back all the time. I wouldn't want to set God off, too.

Rhonda: You won't set him off. You can tell him everything you have to hold back from everyone else, and ...

Beth: *(interrupting)* And he won't strike me dead?

Rhonda: *(laughing)* No. And he won't love you any less.

Beth: That's not saying much. My ex won't love me any less either, 'cause he doesn't love me at all.

Rhonda: With God it's just the opposite. God's love for you can't get any bigger because he already loves you with everything that he is.

Beth: *(shaking her head)* Not me. I haven't kept my end of the deal. I never went to church. I never got my life together. I don't deserve it.

Rhonda: None of us deserve it. But that never stops him. He loves you. He even died for you.

Beth: Why? *(softens)* Why would he ever do that for me?

Rhonda: Because of his grace.

(Beth lowers her head slightly to her hand as she considers Rhonda's words. Rhonda watches with compassion. The lights go down.)

That It May Be Well With You

"That It May Be Well With You" explores honoring one's parents and being an honorable parent. It is a humorous look at misconceptions of honor as they make their way through three generations of an Israelite family. The sketch is based on the fifth commandment found in Exodus 20:12. Related topics include passages on family relationships that call for children to obey parents and parents to keep from exasperating their children, as well as the effect of our attitudes and actions on future generations.

Cast

Therapist — Mr. Levi, the family counselor in the Israelite camp

Grandfather — Mr. Benjamin

Mother — daughter of Mr. Benjamin and mother of teenage boy

Josh — teenage son

Setting And Costumes

On the stage, four chairs are arranged with one of the chairs facing two others, a fourth is off to the side. This is the tent of the family counselor of the Israelite camp. There may be weathered brown canvas on the wall behind to suggest a tent, but it is not necessary. A sign on the stage reads: "Mr. Levi, Family Therapist."

Each member of the cast is dressed in a draped, robe-like garment to suggest the time period.

Props

Four primitive looking chairs, benches, or stools — should be light enough to be moved easily

Sign — "Mr. Levi, Family Therapist"

(Therapist is sitting in his tent/office. He sits on the bench or chair that is facing the other three. Grandfather walks up, shakes his head as though he doesn't want to be there, and looks into the tent.)

Grandfather: You the doctor?

Therapist: I'm the counselor.

Grandfather: Good enough.

Therapist: Are you Mr. Benjamin?

Grandfather: Yeah, I'm only here because my daughter wanted me to come.

(Therapist nods his head.)

Grandfather: But don't tell her I was here. I think all of you therapist, counselor, family, whatever-you-are people are quacks. I only came so when she throws it up in my face again I can tell her I tried it and it didn't work. I tell her over and over to listen to me, do what I say, respect me. Been telling her for forty years. *(smiles)* And then when Moses came down the mountain with those tablets ... he just proved I was right. The only thing Moses has done right since he brought us out into this desert to die. He said, "Honor your father."

Therapist: And your mother.

Grandfather: *(waves his hand as if Therapist's statement is irrelevant)* Oh, yeah, you guys always have to talk about mothers. *(in a mocking tone)* What was your relationship like with your mother? Well I can tell you about my mother. She was just like my daughter and just like my wife. Women! *(shakes his head)* So Doctor, you haven't earned your money, yet. How do I make my daughter honor me?

84

Therapist: Mr. Benjamin, are you honorable?

Grandfather: *(leans forward with a disgusted look)* Am I honorable? I'm old! Of course I'm honorable. In Egypt, I cut blocks out of stone. I made bricks without straw, and I did it all walking miles with no shoes. Then I left Egypt to follow Moses while he bumbles across the desert. No plans for food. No plans for water. Carrying our own shelter. *(with sarcasm)* Letting God provide. *(moves arms as if indicating the whole campful of people)* I've worked hard and put up with these people my whole life. Of course I'm honorable! *(stands up)* And I don't have to listen to anyone question me, *(spits the words out)* especially you child, marriage, therapist, family, whatever-you-are.

(Grandfather leaves the tent as Mother is coming in.)

Mother: Dad? *(surprised)*

(Grandfather is too angry to speak to her. He just looks at her and huffs away.)

Mother: *(talks compulsively until she leaves)* I see my Dad came in. I just try to tune him out. Do you know what I mean? I'm so tired of his complaining and his stories. *(mimics her dad)* "In Egypt, I made bricks with no straw, and I did it all with no shoes." When we get to the promised land, if we ever really do, he and Mom will probably find some reason not to go in. It won't be good enough for them. The grapes won't be purple enough, the people won't be friendly enough, the milk and honey won't flow in the right direction. I don't know. They'll think of something. They're so stubborn, they'd rather wander around in the desert for years instead of ... Oh well, enough of that. *(sits down)* What I really came to talk about was my parents ... my dad. *(She takes a breath. Therapist interrupts.)*

Therapist: And the commandments?

85

Mother: *(leans forward)* You are so perceptive. You know, I told my husband just this morning, or maybe last night, I said, "Dr. Levi is so perceptive. He'll know what to do about Dad and about Josh." Josh is our son. You've probably seen him. You know Josh was so talkative as a child, but now I say we need to have a family talk. I make him sit down and my husband too, but at the end of the hour I'm the only one who's talked. I don't understand it. So anyway what were we talking about?

Therapist: Your parents?

Mother: My parents. So Moses comes down from the mountain and reads these commandments from God. Do you know what one of them said?

Therapist: Honor your ...

Mother: *(interrupts)* It said honor your father and mother so that it may be well with you in the new land. Do you know my father? Have you met him? I guess you have, I just saw him here. He is the most stubborn, obnoxious, complaining person I know. And the worse thing ... Do you want to know what the worse thing is? He dominates every conversation. If he were in here talking to you, he would have been talking this whole time ... Nonstop! I love him, but I don't think I honor him, and I certainly don't want to be like him.

(Josh walks up to the tent. He walks a little slumped over, his hands in his robe pocket. He looks very bored.)

Mother: *(looks at Josh)* Josh, where have you been? You know what time our appointment was.

Josh: *(enters the tent, still slumped over, mumbles when he speaks)* At least I came. Dad wouldn't even come.

Mother: *(slightly irritated at first and then quickly forgets)* Come sit over here. Dr. Levi can you stand up for a minute? *(begins rearranging the benches)* I've been reading and it's very important where everyone sits for these kinds of sessions. *(When she is finished, Mother is sitting where Therapist was. Josh and Therapist sit next to each other facing her. She drags one more bench in.)* And we need an empty seat, too. I don't remember why, but we need it in therapy, and I think in Passover. *(She sits down. Speaks to Josh as though to a young child.)* Josh, Dr. Levi and I have been talking about our family. Do you remember the commandments from Moses?

Josh: *(shrugs and mumbles)* I don't know.

Mother: Josh, try to think. Do you remember now?

(Josh shrugs and mumbles again.)

Mother: Remember when you were little and I taught you to try to think harder by doing this with your hands *(puts a hand on each side of her face)* and saying, "Think Joshy, think?" Why don't you try that?

Josh: *(rolls eyes)* Mom!

Mother: *(in a warning tone)* Joshy.

(Josh looks down.)

Mother: Come on Joshy, I'll do it with you.

Josh and Mother: *(Josh shakes his head, but puts his hands on his face and mumbles something as his Mother says with him)* Think Joshy, think.

Mother: Much better. Now what were we trying to think of? Oh yes, Moses coming down the mountain. Josh do you remember that?

Josh: *(mumbles)* Which time?

Mother: What Josh? Can you say it again? This is so wonderful, we're talking together. Tell me again, Joshy. Do you remember when Moses came down the mountain?

Josh: *(irritated, answers loudly emphasizing each word)* Which time?

Mother: *(suddenly remembers something and is embarrassed, so she talks faster to try to steer clear of it)* Joshy, he only gave us the commandments one time. You know that. Remember? He had those tablets. He read honor your ...

Josh: *(angrily interrupts)* Mom, you know what I mean! The first time Moses came down from the mountain he saw you and your friends dancing around that golden calf that Aaron made. He threw down the stone tablets and they broke. Remember Mom? You were the one dancing around with the bells.

Mother: Josh, that's no way to talk to me. See Dr. Levi, that's what I'm talking about. There is no respect ... and the lies ... It's the lies I just can't ...

Josh: *(interrupts)* Mom, you don't need to cover it up. He was there. He saw you. I saw you. Dad saw you. Grandfather saw you. Everyone saw you.

Mother: *(She is speechless for the first time. Standing up, she looks at both of them then starts talking faster than ever.)* Well Dr. Levi, thank you. This has been so helpful. As I told my husband, you are perceptive, so perceptive. I'll just leave you to talk with Joshy now ... I think that's where the real problem is. *(Mother leaves and talks all the way out the door)* I know some of my neighbors saw the golden calf ... or ... whatever that idol was. I didn't get over there that day ... mostly stay to myself, mind my own business.

(It is very quiet. There is a long pause while Josh and Therapist give each other a sympathetic look. The therapist shakes his head and lowers it into his hands. Josh walks over to Therapist and puts his arm around his shoulder to comfort him and commiserate.)

When All You've Got ... Is Gone

When our loss is so intense that we lose even our hope, we have a shepherd who can find it. This monologue makes real to the audience the feeling of lost hope.

Cast
A man who appears to be no younger than late thirties. He is honest, direct, and hovering between hope and hopelessness.

Setting And Costumes
This monologue works best with the actor dressed in simple clothes on an empty stage.

Props
No props needed

I'd heard the stories when I was little. Parables they're called. Things were lost, they were searched for and then ... and then they were found. Coins, sheep ... even sons. They hoped, they searched, and they hoped ... and they found. But what about when hope is the thing you lost? What do you do then?

I don't quite know when my hope got lost or where, and it wasn't the first thing I lost. First, I lost a son. I don't wait for him to come walking up the road and ask to be my son again. He died. I lost him to AIDS. But I'd really lost him long before that to my anger.

Then I lost a coin. No, not a coin, a whole bank account of them. My business partner made sure they were lost so well I'll never find them. It was sometime after that I reached for my hope and ... it was gone, too. And when that's gone, there's not much left.

I heard once that hope is the anchor of the soul. I guess it's true because after that I started drifting. And now *I'm* that lost son

91

... except in those stories, those parables, the son comes home on his own ... and I wouldn't even know where to go. I'm afraid I'm more like the sheep who just stands out there in the cold waiting for its shepherd to lift it onto his shoulders and carry it home.

I don't know if I can ever hope again, but if there's any shred of hope still alive in me ... I'm going to hope for a shepherd like that.

Just Look At Yourself!

Because of a wrong turn in space and in time, two deliverymen leave a very large screen television at a caveman's doorstep. He watches with growing discontent as the actors step out of their commercials and into his living room to tell him the things he lacks. "Just Look At Yourself!" deals with discontentment and the messages we receive about who we are and what we need.

Cast

Caveman — communicates with grunts and gestures, but very expressive

Cavewoman — independent for a cavewoman

Deliveryman 1 — frustrated with his bumbling partner, but a little bumbling himself

Deliveryman 2 — bumbling and incompetent

Aunt Sally — grandmotherly looking, artificially sweet

Workoutman — macho

Mr. Reamum — condescending

Psychic — female, phony

Diamond Man — not a speaking part, to keep cast smaller it's best to double this part with another one.

Diamond Woman — not a speaking part, to keep cast smaller it's best to double this part with another one.

Diamond Commercial Voice — male, voice only, a commercial voice.

Jingle singer/Musician (optional) — as each commercial starts and ends a short jingle can be sung or a short theme played on a keyboard/synthesizer.

Setting And Costumes

There is some type of primitive couch or chair on stage, maybe some rocks, a cave entrance, plants, animal skins, and the like. This is the home of the caveman and cavewoman.

Caveman and Cavewoman are dressed in animal print cavepeople clothes. The Deliveryman 1 and 2 are dressed in work shirts and pants or overalls with some type of logo on the back. Aunt Sally has her hair back in a bun, she is dressed grandmotherly in a dress and apron as if she has just stepped out of her kitchen. Workoutman is dressed in workout clothes. Mr. Reamum is dressed in a suit. Psychic is dressed in a loose, flowing blouse and skirt with lots of long jewelry and beads. Diamond Man is dressed in a suit. Diamond Woman is dressed nicely.

Props

Large frame made of wood, possibly cardboard; it is the frame of the television. It needs to stand up and must be big enough for people to step out of. A piece of material covers the opening. There is a slit where the commercial characters step through to talk to Caveman. On the bottom are knobs and buttons, like on a television.

Paper for Deliveryman to pull from his pocket

Bag of cookies for Aunt Sally

Contract and pen for Workoutman

Suit on a hanger for Mr. Reamum, this is in addition to the suit he wears

Two leather pouches for Caveman's and Cavewoman's purses

Small stones for Cavewoman's money

"Rock" for Caveman to use as couch

Necklace made of primitive looking beads

Shopping bags from department stores with purchases inside

"Diamond" necklace

Additional Notes

As each commercial appears on the caveman's television, a short jingle can be sung or played. The number of actors may be reduced by having actors play several parts.

───────────

(Caveman, through a series of grunts and gestures, tells his wife good-bye in front of the door of their cave. Cavewoman needs money. She holds up her leather pouch and turns it over to indicate she is out. Caveman takes out his leather pouch and pours

some stones from it. He gives them to her. She hugs him good-bye and happily leaves. They both smile. He has the day to himself to relax. He looks around as if admiring the day and stretches contentedly. He settles down on his caveman rock or couch with a luxurious yawn. Deliveryman 1 and 2 walk on stage carrying the huge television. Caveman is out of their sight.)

Deliveryman 1: I still think we took a wrong turn somewhere. *(It is obvious by their tone that the argument has been going on a long time.)*

Deliveryman 2: We didn't take a wrong turn.

Deliveryman 1: Remember when the pavement ended and you kept going? You were supposed to turn right.

(There is an angry silence. They are still carrying the television.)

Deliveryman 1: Look at this place. It looks like we stepped back into the Stone Age. Do you really think someone here ordered an eighty-inch television?

Deliveryman 2: This is the place. Knock on the door.

Deliveryman 1: There's not a door.

Deliveryman 2: Then yell for someone. *(pulls a paper from his pocket)* Says the name's Rutherford.

Deliveryman 1: *(yells)* Mr. Rutherford ... Mr. Rutherford?

(Caveman is afraid of them. He is peeking at them from the other side of the stage. He is obviously not Mr. Rutherford. Deliverymen do not see him.)

Deliveryman 2: Let's just leave it.

Deliveryman 1: Leave it?

Deliveryman 2: They knew we were coming. They'll be home.

Deliveryman 1: You don't even know if this is the right place. We can't just leave it.

Deliveryman 2: It's the right place. Let's go!

(Deliveryman 1 throws up his arms in frustration. Deliveryman 1 and 2 walk away in different directions.)

Deliveryman 1: Jack, the truck's over here.

(Deliveryman 2 turns and follows Deliveryman 1 off the stage. When they are gone, Caveman tiptoes from his hiding place. He curiously examines the television trying to look inside and push the buttons. One button causes the screen to light up. Aunt Sally appears in the television. Caveman jumps back, afraid but intrigued.)

Aunt Sally: *(holds a cookie and a cookie bag and talks in a too-sweet voice)* Aunt Sally's cookies will fill your home with the warmth of fresh baked cookies. It's just like having Aunt Sally in your kitchen.

(Caveman looks hungrily at the cookies.)

Aunt Sally: *(steps toward him out of the television screen, now talking in an accusing voice)* Do you want these cookies?

(Caveman grunts expectantly and nods.)

Aunt Sally: Of course you do. Look at you. Are you happy? Of course you're not. Here all by yourself while your wife shops. She just leaves you here alone. What kind of a lonely, miserable life is that? Of course you need a cookie. You need the whole bag. *(She hands him the bag. He takes it gratefully. She smiles sweetly again* *and goes back into the television.)* It's just like having Aunt Sally in your kitchen. *(exits)*

(Caveman happily munches his cookies.)

Workoutman: *(appears in the television next, he has a big smile and a pose)* For just $65 a month, Power Gym can give you the body you wish you had.

(Caveman looks at himself, shrugs, and eats another cookie.)

Workoutman: *(steps out of the television and looks disgustedly at Caveman and his cookies)* Look at yourself! You're a weakling!

(Caveman looks at himself in a confused sort of way.)

Workoutman: Are you happy with this body? *(grabs Caveman's arm and holds it up)* Okay, let's see that muscle. Come on. *(gets the Caveman to flex his muscle)* Now look at this muscle. *(flexes his own muscle)* Come on feel it. Now feel yours again.

(Caveman compares their muscles, then slumps down on his rock.)

Workoutman: You need to sign up.

(Caveman grunts dejectedly and nods.)

Workoutman: *(pulls out a contract and pen)* I have a contract here.

(Caveman takes the pen and tries to figure out what to do with it. Finally he puts it in his mouth.)

Workoutman: *(takes the pen and wipes it off)* Here, I'll do it for you. *(signs the contract and begins talking quickly)* Now that's only $150. First month, last month, and a Power Gym T-shirt. *(climbs back into the television, turns to his television audience, and says)* At Power Gym you can get the body you wish you had.

(Caveman is looking at his muscles as the next commercial begins.)

Mr. Reamum: *(with a superior attitude)* At Reamum Brothers, we care about your image. Why settle for a suit, when you can have an exquisite wardrobe experience? *(While still in the television, he squints out at Caveman as though he can't believe his eyes. He steps out of the television.)* Look at yourself. You're a Neanderthal.

(Caveman smiles and grunts and nods.)

Mr. Reamum: *(shakes his head in disgust)* Do you know how long that suit's been out of style? Listen, you keep wearing that and the business world will pass you right by. You'll find yourself sitting out on the sidewalk with your briefcase and your laptop.

(Caveman is confused.)

Mr. Reamum: *(hands Caveman a suit)* Here. This one's your color. I'm sure you can't afford it. No one can really, but you need it. It will make you happy. *(steps back into the television)* Why settle for a suit when you can have an exquisite wardrobe experience? *(exits)*

Psychic: *(appears on television)* Do you want to be happy?

(Caveman grunts and nods.)

Psychic: Do you need to know where your life is headed?

(Caveman grunts and nods.)

Psychic: You deserve to enjoy your life without worrying about the future.

(Caveman grunts and nods.)

Psychic: At Psychic Helpers we take the worry out of your future. Our trained psychics are waiting for your call. Just pick up the phone and dial 1-800-Know Now.

(Caveman looks around but doesn't have a phone.)

Psychic: *(Steps out of television and looks around for the phone)* You don't even *have* a phone do you?

(Caveman shakes his head.)

Psychic: I ... could sense that. *(stares off into space as though "seeing" something)* I sense that you want to be happy.

(Caveman nods and grunts longingly.)

Psychic: I see so many possibilities in your future.

(Caveman grunts and puts his hand to his heart as though hearing what he's always wanted to hear.)

Psychic: *(sees Caveman's taking her seriously and decides to risk a prediction)* There was a time when you thought of starting a business.

(Caveman drops hand from his heart. His face falls. His grunt sounds like, "Huh?")

Psychic: *(flustered)* It ... It works better over the phone. *(steps quickly back into the television and smiles)* Take the worry out of your future, and dial 1-800-Know Now. *(exits)*

(Caveman slumps down on his rock. Then he slaps at the buttons on the television. It turns off. Cavewoman enters just after the television goes off. She doesn't notice the television at first. She is carrying big bags from various department stores and through grunts and gestures tries to tell him she stepped through a time

99

*warp and into a shopping mall [or something like that]. Caveman
is distressed. He looks through her bags. He holds up the leather
pouch as though asking how much it cost. Then Cavewoman spots
the television. She stops and stares. She walks over and begins
pushing buttons. Caveman tries to get her away from it. He mimics what happens when you push the button: People step out, be-
rate you, and take your money. Cavewoman refuses to leave it alone.
They argue. Caveman waves the empty leather pouch in her face.
Finally Caveman drags or carries Cavewoman away while she
struggles to get to the television. As they leave, the Cavewoman
manages to hit the bottom of the television. It lights up again. Diamond Man and Diamond Woman appear on it. He is putting a
necklace around her neck. They hold the pose and smile once the
necklace is on.)*

Diamond Commercial Voice: Tell her you'd marry her all over
again. Nothing says it like diamonds.

*(Cavewoman, just before she exits the stage, looks at the primitive
beads around her neck then looks at Caveman and gives a discon-
tented sigh. Caveman answers with an angry grunt.)*

A Risky Gamble

In "A Risky Gamble" we listen in on a conversation in a casino. The way to the most money with the least effort is discussed. Attitudes on work, wealth, tithing, gambling, and get rich quick schemes are examined. Throughout the drama we watch the consequences of the characters' gambling habits.

Cast

Gambler 1 — only seen as he enters the stage. The entire sketch is spent behind the "slot machine." We only hear his voice and see the money and objects he drops through.

Gambler 2 — only seen as he enters the stage. The entire sketch is spent behind the "slot machine." We only hear his voice and see the money and objects he drops through.

Setting And Costumes

The setting is a casino. The slot machine is on the stage. The audience does not see the actors. Instead they see the money and objects that are pushed through the slots. They slide down a ramp into trash cans.

Gamblers wear casual clothes.

Props

Slot machine — large piece of wood, cardboard, or a cardboard box with two slits cut in it for slots

Large amount of coins and bills

Two keys, each attached to a large car-shaped keychain to show a car has been lost to gambling

Two keys, each attached to a large house-shaped keychain to show a house has been lost to gambling

Watches

Family picture for each of the gamblers large enough to be seen by audience as it slides down ramp into the trash can

(Gambler 1 enters and goes to the "slot machine." Begins to put money through. Sometimes coins, sometimes single bills, sometimes wads of bills.)

Gambler 2: *(enters at the other side of the "slot machine" and goes behind it)* This machine taken?

Gambler 1: No, go ahead.

Gambler 2: Thanks. *(begins to put money through the slot)* This place is great.

Gambler 1: Yeah. It's the only place you can come in for free. *(drops money through the slot)* Those amusement parks you pay fifty bucks just to get in.

Gambler 2: Here you make money. How much've you won so far?

Gambler 1: Five bucks. How 'bout you?

Gambler 2: Nothing yet. I just got here. But I'm planning to take home plenty. I just got paid. I cashed my check before I got here. I brought half of it.

Gambler 1: *(surprised)* Half of it? You can afford to gamble with half of your paycheck?

Gambler 2: Not really, but I see it as an investment. If you do this right you can quit work.

Gambler 1: You're kidding?

Gambler 2: Nope. I'm going to.

Gambler 1: You're going to quit work and gamble full time?

Gambler 2: Not yet, but soon. I figure there are plenty of people who like to work. So let them. Why should I work if I can get rich doing this?

Gambler 1: That's pretty risky. What if you lose everything?

(Money, keys, watches, and family pictures are being dropped through the slot.)

Gambler 2: I might, but what if I win everything? Here's my philosophy: life is one big slot machine. Everything is random chance. You put in your money, pull the handle, and get what you get. People look for rhyme and reason, order, they look for God ... but they won't find any of it. Chance is all there is. So, I might as well make it work for me instead of against me.

Gambler 1: That's an interesting theory. Not as crazy as my friend Ted's ideas though.

Gambler 2: What are Ted's ideas? Does he bet on horses or something? Horses are pretty crazy.

Gambler 1: No, he's going to church.

Gambler 2: Church?

Gambler 1: Yeah, and he's started tithing.

Gambler 2: What's that?

Gambler 1: Well you know when you go to church and they take an offering?

Gambler 2: Yeah, I guess. I try not to go there when they do that.

Gambler 1: Me neither, but anyway, he puts in ten percent out of everything he makes.

Gambler 2: No way. Ten percent? How does he pay his bills and take care of his family? He must be really rich to put in ten percent.

Gambler 1: No, he's not. He works with me and makes about what I do. And believe me, it just barely stretches.

Gambler 2: So what's his plan? Is it some kind of high-risk investment program the church is doing or something? How does he plan to make his money back?

Gambler 1: He doesn't. That's what's so crazy about it. He says he's trusting God to help him with what he needs. He says God promises to take care of him.

Gambler 2: *(dropping in a wad of bills as he speaks)* So he just puts in his money, without getting anything back except a promise from God?

Gambler 1: Told you he's crazy.

Gambler 2: That's a pretty risky gamble.

Gambler 1: That's for sure.

Gambler 2: Well, I'll see you. I'm going to try over there for a while.

Gambler 1: Okay. I'm going to find the ATM machine. Good luck.

You Think I'm What?

Are you entitled to your employer's paper clips, cars, time, coffee, and pencils for your personal use? This man seems to think so. He is insulted (and extremely convicted) by the audience's perception that he is stealing. We hear his rationalizations.

Cast

A man (or woman) with the demeanor of one who knows he (or she) is doing wrong but refuses to admit to it.

Setting And Costumes

A desk is in the middle of the stage. On it are items that would be typically found on a desk in a workplace.

The man or woman wears a coat with large pockets.

Props

Desk
Briefcase
Pens
Pencils
Paper clips
Paper
Computer disks
Other work-desk items

(The employee is standing behind the desk. He or she is putting pens, pencils, paper clips, paper, computer disks, and so on, in a briefcase and in pockets. Finally picks up another pen, looks for a place to put it and sticks it behind ear. Looks up as if noticing audience.)

Oh, hi. *(pauses and looks at audience with a guilty and then offended look)* You think I'm what? Stealing? No! Stealing is taking things that don't belong to you. Believe me, this stuff is mine.

105

I have a right to all of it, plus the desk light from the storage room and the can of coffee from the break room. *(pauses to look at audience and then continues defensively)* Well, we were out of coffee at home, and it's late. I don't want to stop at the store. Besides they have ten other cans here. If I don't get my coffee in the morning I'm useless until noon. If they expect me to show up here at eight in the morning, believe me, I need the coffee.

Talk about stealing, do you know how many years this company has stolen from my life? And it's been over two years since my last raise. You know, those *(in an irritated tone)* performance reviews? Everyone always has to check up on everyone these days. This time my boss said I don't use time productively. Last year it was too many personal phone calls and too many personal miles on the company car. Well excuuuuuse me for having a personal life. They give you a paycheck and think it gives them the right to tell you what to do.

Let me tell you, they'd be in big trouble if I ever left, but the only way I can afford to stay here is to *(picks up more supplies and stuffs them into coat)* increase my benefits. They should just be grateful I'm here at all. Without me they'd be losing money left and right. *(begins to walk off stage with the load of supplies and then turns to assure audience of his/her innocence)* I'm doing them a favor. Really.

Seeds?

God has big dreams for our lives. He wants to plant in us the seeds that grow into fruitfulness and powerful faith. We can participate with him in this planting or we can spend our efforts on things that yield no fruit. Cindy's and Susan's gardens show us the importance of allowing God to plant in our life rather than just spending our energy managing the weeds that come up when we fail to plant.

Cast

Susan — experienced gardener, eager to begin her garden and to share her love of gardening with her neighbor

Cindy — caught up in all the accessories of gardening rather than gardening itself, she misses the point

Setting And Costumes

This sketch takes place in neighboring backyard gardens.

Both women are dressed for work in their gardens. Cindy has much more stylish gardening clothes than Susan since she has no intention of getting them dirty.

Props

Gardening gloves
Hat
Pot
Watering Can
Shovel
Basket of vegetables
Additional plants or gardening supplies can be set around on the stage if desired.

(Cindy and Susan are each in their own backyard, preparing to garden.)

Cindy: *(putting on and admiring her new gardening gloves, notices her neighbor, Susan, is also in her garden)* Good morning, Susan.

Susan: Oh, hi! Cindy, I'm so excited. I'm going to start planting this morning. *(notices all the gardening equipment)* Are you going to have a garden this year?

Cindy: Yes. I've been looking for a place to put it.

Susan: Where were you thinking? *(looks around at Cindy's yard)* Over there by the fence might work well ... or ...

Cindy: *(holds up a little pot)* I was thinking ... in here.

Susan: Or ... in there. *(a little embarrassed for Cindy and her small garden, so changes the subject)* Hey, did you hear about the sale at Orchard Supply? *(gets excited)* All their seeds and bulbs and bare root roses and trees are on sale. I spent a small fortune this morning. See, I have this dream of a backyard oasis. I'm planting roses all along this fence, and trellises here with honeysuckle, a vegetable garden over here, and a tree in that corner that will shade a little bench with ... *(realizes she's going on and on)* I'm sorry. I get so excited with all my big dreams. So, the short version of the story is, go to Orchard Supply; they're having a great sale.

Cindy: I went last night. That's what inspired me to have a garden this year.

Susan: What did you find?

Cindy: I found this great watering can. *(shows watering can)* I feel like a gardener just holding it. It has the same sunflower pattern as my wallpaper. And I found these gloves, *(holds out her gloved hands)* and a matching hat ... *(shows hat)* Oh, and a little, nickel-plated shovel. *(shows shovel)* It's so cute.

Susan: Well the shovel should come in handy for planting.

Cindy: It's so pretty though, I think I might hang it on my wall. I also found an umbrella to keep the sun off me while I work, and some special gardeners' hand cleaner in case I get my hands dirty, and ...

Susan: *(excited)* Did you go down the aisle with the fruit trees? I'm planting an apple tree, an apricot tree, and a cherry tree. I can already picture them five years from now full of ripe fruit ... not to mention the pies. There I go dreaming again. I can't wait to get started.

Cindy: I know what you mean. I've been waiting all morning. The truck should be here any minute.

Susan: The truck?

Cindy: The delivery truck to bring the rest of my gardening stuff.

Susan: Trees?

Cindy: No, a wheelbarrow that matches the watering can; and a gardener's cart with a cup holder, a place to put a cell phone, and a built-in CD player, and ...

Susan: *(getting concerned for her friend's garden)* Cindy, what are you going to plant in your ... pot? What kind of seeds did you buy?

Cindy: *(a completely puzzled look)* Seeds? I didn't buy any seeds.

(Cindy and Susan exit. Susan enters carrying a basket of vegetables. Cindy enters carrying nothing.)

Susan: Hi, Cindy. I thought you might like some of this.

Cindy: *(takes the basket)* Thanks. Where'd you get all this?

Susan: From my garden.

Cindy: Oh. *(shades her eyes and looks over toward Susan's garden)* Did it turn out like you were hoping? I remember you had such big dreams for it in the spring.

Susan: It did. I'm still working on it, of course, and I can't wait for my trees to start bearing fruit in a few years. Here, I'll show you.

(Susan and Cindy walk toward Susan's garden.)

Cindy: I don't think I'll garden next year. I just spent all my time pulling weeds, and other than weeds, nothing grew. And nothing at all grew in here. *(holds up pot)*

Susan: I pulled quite a few weeds myself, but pretty soon the plants began taking over and there were less weeds to pull. What kind of things did you end up planting?

Cindy: I didn't plant anything.

Susan: What kinds of things would you like to grow?

Cindy: I never really thought about it. I don't know.

Susan: Tell you what. Today, you imagine the garden you would like. Tomorrow, we'll go pick out the seeds.

Cindy: *(picks up the basket)* Thanks, Susan.

(Both exit.)